PRAISE FOR *LOV*

"In this marvelously insightful, beautifully written book, Karen Aberle addresses one of the central issues of our time: the constant struggle, especially for women, to develop a fully satisfying life for themselves in a loving relationship with another."

RICHARD OGLE, AUTHOR OF *SMART WORLD: BREAKTHROUGH CREATIVITY AND THE SCIENCE OF NEW IDEAS*

"Karen Aberle has given us a simple yet extraordinary way to see ourselves in the dance of life. She's a world-class performer and teacher whose openness and humanity, distinctions and practices inspire appreciation for all of our failures and an eagerness to give love another chance at greatness."

CAROLE HYATT, AUTHOR OF *THE WOMEN'S SELLING GAME* AND *WHEN SMART PEOPLE FAIL*

"In some cultures, the poet is considered a shaman; Karen Aberle is poet, shaman, and teacher who invests us with a way of thinking, deepens our language tools, and helps us overcome life-long habits of thought and action that stand in the way of relationship, leadership and creative collaboration."

CHRISTINE KELLY, SENIOR LECTURER, MIT SLOANE SCHOOL OF MANAGEMENT

"Karen offers an approach to the mystery of love and relatedness, that in its very practicality moves one toward the truth and honesty that is crucial to crossing the threshold to the experience of the heart, where the song of the world can be heard, both individually and in relationship."

BARRY WILLIAMS, M.DIV., PSY.D., DIPLOMATE JUNGIAN ANALYST AND FOUNDING MEMBER OF THE C.G. JUNG INSTITUTE OF SANTA FE

"Karen Aberle's invitation for us to put aside our assumptions about what it takes to be in a healthy, loving, committed relationship is nothing short of exciting and brilliant!"

SALLY CHAPDELAINE, RNCS, COUPLES/FAMILY THERAPIST

LOVE'S INVISIBLE DANCE

Karen Aberle

To Janet ~
A pleasure to
meet you ~ you light up
the world.
Karen

LOVE'S INVISIBLE DANCE

the 7 keys to authentic, joyful and
lasting relationship

Karen Aberle

LOVE'S INVISIBLE DANCE
the 7 keys to authentic, joyful, and lasting relationship

Edgefield Press

Cover Design by Verónica Cortés Montiglio

For more information about the author and this book, please
visit: www.karenaberle.com

ISBN 13 978-1-7324089-0-6 Paperback
ISBN 13 978-1-7324089-1-3 Kindle

For the next seven generations.

Dance me to your beauty with a burning violin
Dance me through the panic till I'm gathered safely in
Lift me like an olive branch and be my homeward dove
Dance me to the end of love

Leonard Cohen

Appreciation and Gratitude

To my mother who bore me, did your best to raise me, and taught me about truth and beauty, lies and courage. To my ancestors whose histories of love and loss live in my DNA. To life itself, I am humbled by the brilliance and mystery of this world. Cristián Valenzuela, my co-conspirator, my 'we,' my joy. I can hardly believe the amazing life we have created together. Lael Brodsky and Lauren Iozzo, my precious daughters, you grew me up and loved me through all my craziness. I am so proud of who you have become. Peter Brodsky, my almost son, I'm so grateful for your constant support, generosity, and socially conscious heart. Patric Iozzo, my first love, father of my children, rest in peace, with so much appreciation for our time together. Paul Gold, you made me a princess and dethroned me, and in the process, gave me everything I needed. Lisa Gansky, you taught me how to move from "I don't know" to creation and put me on the path of learning. You will always be the smartest and funniest part of me. Inés Montiglio, María Jesús Valenzuela, and my Chilean family, the finest example of acceptance, grace in conflict, and care.

Werner Erhard, you showed me my responsibility for my life, crises and all. Fernando Flores, you taught me how to think new thoughts, introduced me to the moves of the dance, and made my career possible with your genius. Julio Olalla, the master of compassionate coaching. Eliot Cowan, David Wiley, Don Lupe Gonzales Rios, Don Jose Sandoval, and the Huichol people of San Andrés Cohamiata, the sacred sites of my pilgrimages, and the shamans of the Sacred Fire

Community, you showed me the interconnected web of the world, taught me to listen with my heart, what it takes to sit in council, and incredible laughter.

Richard Ogle, you taught me to discover who I am and what I think by writing and how to be coherent about it. You've been incredibly generous and dedicated to this project and my life. One of my greatest joys is to think with you. The extraordinary business leaders with whom I've worked – Jim Heneghan, Todd Stewart, Kim Craig-Woodworth, Michael Hills, and Ed Mazzella. David Kelly, throughout our twenty plus years together, your trust and love allowed me to learn as I taught. Mel Auston, for our early years of collaboration. Kening Zhu, you taught me so much while you generously edited this book, opened my eyes to simplicity and ease, and put a world of Zen in me. Mark Malatesta, this book took shape under your tutelage. My agent, Lisa Hagan, you took a risk and jumped with a first-time author with a big idea. Farah White for bringing me into the world of video. Verónica Cortés for the exquisite cover. Chuck Finkle and Mario Coloma turned my ideas into art. Mary Lou Kayser, my book's midwife. Tucker Farley, Achebe Powell, Anita Mandl, Sally Fisher, and Beverly Grasso, my accomplices in learning about real beauty and aging with grace. Sally Chapdelaine for your balance, love, and constant presence. Angelica Sgouros, Marsha Shenk, Lucy Freedman, Deborah Naish, Ron Williams, BJ Dockweiler, Chris Kelly, Andrea Spica, Heather Goodstein, Hylke Faber, Carolina Galaz, Katarina and Richard Diss, and my vast network of friends and clients who read my drafts, kept me going with your enthusiasm, and kicked my ass as was needed.

I am a blessed woman.

Contents

Introduction

"In the universe, there are things that are known and things that are unknown, and in between, there are doors."

–William Blake

KEITH AND SUZANNE are getting divorced. They've been together 10 years and have a four-year old daughter. He's a management consultant, having just self-published his first book. His income vacillates. He's not accruing wealth. The book cost him substantially. At the same time, he values the investment in expanding his learning and his identity. She is a Ph.D. government employee who is less adventurous, admits that she longs for stability and comfort, and hasn't tolerated well his inconsistent income. In the battle about getting a "real" job, he says he feels as though he is shrinking. After a lot of struggle and mixed emotion, with a mutual concern for their child, they are moving on and working out the details.

Keith and Suzanne are a perfect example of love undone. They lost that loving feeling. Theirs is a common story. In dopamine-flooded euphorias, they were enthralled with their differences at the same time as being remarkably attuned to the other. Vanished was the effortlessness of mutual pleasure – when giving to the other was a gift to themselves. Inevitably, when the heat cooled and they landed on the quarry-cold ground of personal preferences and agendas, unresolved differences and conflict triggered bad moods and diminished sex. "You aren't the person I fell in love with," irreconcilable differences, infidelity, alcohol, abuse, or utter disappointment have become valid and acceptable explanations for canceling the promise of forever.

Today, greater than 50% of marriages end in separation, and an uncountable number limp along out of convenience. With two divorces, I've contributed more than my fair share to that statistic. I would say that betrayal was the basic reason in both cases, significant deceits that came as the result of being unprepared to deal with our difficult truths and thwarted expectations. We simply couldn't make it through the rough parts.

The man I married at 19 decided he was gay right around our seventh anniversary and left me and our two daughters with no financial support. The truth was that he had always struggled with his homosexuality, hoping it would go away. Even as I fell victim to his lies, I didn't give up on love. Appreciating the rashness of my youthful decisions, I was certain that a better love could be found. Three years later he appeared - surely the prince this time – a successful executive, who rescued me from poverty and gave me the life of a princess. I stayed at home with my girls, drove carpool, played tennis, and did a little portrait sculpting on the side. Alas, we couldn't make it through our quarrels, the boredom, and the seven-year challenge of discovering what a jerk the other is. His affair with my best friend was undoubtedly part of the mix. Again I was betrayed. Being victimized was harder this time. I lost both my love and my lifeline. And began to doubt that men could be trusted.

Getting burned a couple of times, it gets harder to keep trying. Many who have failed in relationship sound like my friend Jane, a 70ish NYC psychologist who, after two marriages and one long-term relationship all ended with a betrayal, has given up. She says, "I'm just not good at it. I don't have the strength to go through it again."

I was likely headed in Jane's direction when, at a critical moment, I shared my tale of woe with a teacher who asked me one crucial question that would change the course of my life: Did I hold these betrayals as burdens or gifts? I'd never considered the possibility of a choice.

Either, he said, was a valid interpretation. But burdens are those things we have to put up with in life. Their nature is to wound and weaken us. Gifts, on the other hand, are treasures that strengthen us. To answer, I would have to choose between being an innocent victim to their bad behavior or recognizing that they showed me that there was something important for me to learn. The gifts appeared when I stopped blaming them, took responsibility for my failures, and set about to learn. Thus, good began.

At the time, I didn't realize that my commitment to learning was the first step on a path that would lead me to achieve a new identity, a career, a vibrant 30-year marriage, and perhaps the greatest gift – a new perspective on love. I discovered that love is not something that you find but something you create in an invisible dance of relationship that we've been doing all our lives, unconsciously. The dance is not a metaphor. There is an actual dance going on and once you see it, you can't unsee it. Learning to perform the moves of the dance skillfully – there are only six – enables you to produce alignment, invent the future, establish trust, deepen intimacy, create passion, and generate more satisfaction than you ever dreamed possible.

Let me share something about the events that led to my discovery.

Looking at myself critically, I accepted that my first major failure was never having established an autonomous identity.

I had allowed myself to be entirely dependent upon my husbands. Lack of autonomy was particularly problematic. I needed to produce income sufficient to keep my kids in private school. Truth be told, my sculpture business was never going to support me and my resumé was completely inadequate for a job that would pay me what was required to sustain my lifestyle. I had to figure out how to make me – a mother, with a fine arts education, and eight years in sales and management at a US airline – into a valuable offer in the marketplace. Not having a clue about how to do that, I enrolled in a week-long entrepreneur's workshop and began my redesign.

The course was based in the philosophy of language – how we use words to understand the world, create relationship, coordinate with others to produce results, and invent new things. This workshop gave me an introduction to the mechanics of the dance of relationship.

Like any other dance, there is a leader, a follower, and a unique set of basic moves. The only difference is – this dance doesn't happen with your feet; it takes place in your communication, both verbal and non-verbal. We are always dancing – creating space for one another and moving together – with our colleagues, kids, and the supermarket checker. We dance with people we don't even know – on the bus or on the freeway – with the spider, the rain, and basically, everyone and everything we encounter in life. Amazingly, there are only six basic linguistic moves, ways that express our intentions. With them we create satisfaction, suffering, gratitude, and optimism. Every time we think, speak or listen, we are making a move, either harmoniously or in dissonance. Just like learning the tango, harmony in the dance comes by mastering the moves.

My mind was blown. After my years in corporate America, I was well aware of the cost of widespread communication breakdowns. I could see how learning the six linguistic moves could immediately improve business results. My career decision was immediate as soon as I saw the communication software my teacher had developed based on the moves. I went home and bootstrapped a business with my best friend to distribute the software internationally. The time was right. Personal computers were just becoming an essential office tool.

We hardly knew what we were doing. In those early days, there was no internet, no Microsoft Windows, and PCs were just big boxes with 20 MB hard drives. We turned my dining room into an assembly line, installing modems and floppy drives, loading the software, and selling them as complete communication networks. The market was hungry for what we had to offer.

Training was essential for the users. My job was to teach them. Barely ahead of the curve, if we were to succeed in this new business venture, I'd have to get a lot more competent to be able to teach our clients what I had just learned. Pursuing more in-depth education, I committed to a three-year program to study design – how to move from an idea or a concern for something missing, to manifesting it, and producing satisfaction, in language. My career was off to a great start.

In my third year of that program, a man appeared on the path. A fellow student, Cristián was 14 years my junior, fresh out of a two-year marriage with an infant daughter. We met in a San Francisco dance club when a group of students took a night off for salsa. From the moment I saw him, I knew I had to dance with him. The attraction was irresistible. Even as we acknowledged that a rebound relationship was risky and that he should take time to sort himself out, we couldn't keep away from one another. The "falling in love" endorphins carried us smoothly for about 18 months. Without so much as a substantial disagreement, and believing this time I had truly found Mr. Right, we married. Our best friends gave us five years.

Like clockwork, seven years in, we began to implode. I

was 50 at the time, grieving the loss of my youth and attractiveness. His eyes wandered. Therapy didn't help. Knowing how to perform the six moves competently was insufficient. Something was missing in our dance that I couldn't name. I was existentially lost and unable to find my way back to his embrace. Once again, in the face of "too hard," I could find ample reasons to blame him and end it or take responsibility for making it work.

What was I missing? Where did I fail? Looking for answers, I encountered a Mexican shaman who engaged me in a completely non-intellectual way. The shaman's diagnosis: I had an imbalance – too much mind, not enough heart, and an inability to see my husband. He said that there was an important aspect of myself that I didn't yet know. Accepting his analysis as valid, I followed his prescription – a traditional, indigenous ritual called *vision quest* where I would sit on a mountain alone, fasting for some unspecified number of days, doing nothing and going nowhere.

After a month of preparation – cleansing, fasting, focusing exercises, and a sweat lodge, the shaman led me to a plateau high on a Mexican mountain, and deposited me in a circle of corn no bigger than my bedroom, with a sleeping bag and a tarp. He assured me that I would be safe as long as I stayed within my corn circle. He said that I would know when it was time to descend back down the trail he had blazed for me and that I would find him waiting at the bottom.

Desperately afraid, I was sure I was done for when, not five minutes after the shaman disappeared down the mountain, the birds started eating the corn. My corn!!! My mother's voice filled my head, "Stupid girl, what on earth are you doing, playing like an Indian? You're going to die here." The first night I hid my head beneath my tarp, pleading with a growling animal nearby to stay outside my corn circle. The next, I endured hours of electrical storms and hail and awoke under a blanket of ice, amazed to be alive. Gradually, my gnawing hunger subsided. I lost both my need for food and compulsion to do. I just sat and looked and felt. With no distractions, I began to see my place in an alive and interconnected world.

All of my senses became more acute. I could feel the clouds moving the trees and saw the trees dancing with the rain and all of the insects, birds, and animals who lived there, and they with me. I felt the inhalation and exhalation of the mountain breathing and the heartbeat of an alive Earth. I saw the essential balance and perfection of life, as it was, with no need for change. I was completely in peace, tapped into the universal frequency of joy.

The interconnected nature of life is not new news. Philosophers, religion, and science have long supported the view that we are all related, to each other biologically, and to the earth, chemically. While that had made sense to me intellectually, on the mountain, I actually *experienced* the workings of the giant web of inter-reliance, inter-being in which I live. And it was perfect. Seeing myself as a part of the web, I could not make a single move without care and reverence for the whole. I understood that while I had learned the mechanics of human communication, they were only half of the dance. On their own, this knowledge was insufficient to live harmoniously with another. What I had been missing was the reverence for others as myself.

I descended the mountain elated that I had gotten what I came for. My problem was that I'd held myself as separate. I had operated from the perspective that the world was outside of me, like some backdrop that I could access when I wanted and how I wanted. The source of my schism with Cristián was my incapacity to honor him as he was, as a whole and complete being, doing the best he could to navigate life's unfolding, without needing him to change. I could see that we lost our treasure for one another and our ability to merge in union when we began disdaining each other's frailties and imperfections.,

In sharing my vision with Cristián, he could easily see that our dance had fallen apart when we stopped honoring one another. We'd lasted as long as we had by honoring our marriage vows rather than each other. I declared that he was no longer bound by his long-ago commitment. If we were to continue together we'd have to choose each other anew.

We stood at a crossroads. While I was clear I would choose him as he was, I suspected he wouldn't be so sure. He asked for some time to consider, acknowledging the appeal of falling in love again. After two weeks of quiet contemplation, he said, "I know that finding a new lover would be relatively easy. But what would I do after the heat has cooled and I find myself with someone who is unlikely to love me as much as you do or be as good a friend as you are?" He chose to be my partner. And we both committed to learn how to honor one another amidst the selfishness, fantasies, fear, stupidity, disagreements, conflicts, disappointments, and general messiness of life.

Cristián sought his own vision quest. Our shamans invited us to learn the ways of indigenous culture in a 12-year apprenticeship in the tradition of the Huichol Indians of central Mexico. We made arduous annual pilgrimages and encountered the world beyond our intellect. Through fasting, initiation, and other rituals, we developed our capacity to listen – the key to honor and attunement to all within the web.

As the years passed, we found ourselves more deeply in love and with a joyfulness that became palpable to others. When people began to regularly ask us the secret of our enduring affection, we felt compelled to reconstruct our path and our lessons. Our grounding in the philosophy of language had given us a way to put words to and share the heart teachings of the sacred, the way of creating real union – 'the way of love' in the dance of relationship.

Over the last 20 years, I've taught the dance to thousands

of people in corporate programs on leadership and collaboration in companies such as Comcast, Pfizer, and The Children's Hospital of Philadelphia, and with my husband in community workshops all over the globe. In both venues, participants come away with a newfound ability to co-create their lives, experience oneness, and embrace life's inevitable breakdowns and discord as doorways to greater consciousness.

This book presents the way to more love. Anyone can learn it. And you don't have to get divorced, do a master's in philosophy, or become a shaman.

Because we are always shifting between our self as an individual and ourselves in relationship, the book is divided into two parts. Part One, Preparation for the Dance, focuses on the self. If you're not dancing as you would like, whether you're interested in creating a new relationship or want more juice in the one you have, the first place to look is at yourself and what you bring to the dance. The first three chapters focus on how we create an attractive identity, the moves of the dance, and the way in which you presence honor in your life.

Part Two, The Choreography, details how to execute the moves to establish powerful partnership, build trust, deepen intimacy, engage in conflict, and continuously create passion.

Throughout the book, you will be engaged in a series of fundamental questions that require you to make choices about who you are and how you want to live. You are the god of your creation. You are the one to say what you are doing with this life you've been given. To that end, each chapter concludes with journal questions – a way of defining and refining your vision of a meaningful, well-lived life. For this, you should keep a separate notebook. By setting aside a few minutes each day for reflection, you will immediately increase your sense of peace and satisfaction, clarity about your direction, and make new meaning of your failures.

You will discover that your own path is your greatest

teacher. Daily life becomes extraordinary when you have the capacity to be in the present, appreciate where you are and why, determine if you desire change, and have others to conspire with towards the achievement of your dreams. Satisfaction is possible in every moment.

I invite you to take a journey to your life's fullest expression. Learning the dance of relationship is simple, but not easy. The first step is an authentic commitment to become a great dancer.

Shall we dance?

PART ONE

Preparing to Dance

Be Someone Attractive to Dance With

"She is not truly beautiful but something about her draws the eye."

– George R.R. Martin

W HEN YOU REFLECT on life as an endless stream of encounters, or dances, with others, in each encounter you can see an instantaneous reflex to move – either towards or away from the other, as if in a magnetic field. An invisible energy draws you together or repels you. Attraction is the urge of your whole being to be close to her/him/it/them. Recurrently being drawn to another turns strangers into associates, associates into friends, and friends into partners. It follows, then, that the more attractive you are to others, the greater your social currency and opportunity to choose your dance partners. If you are not dancing as you would like, and with whom you would like, first and foremost, focus your attention on how attractive you are – to yourself.

Sherry is single. She has a great job with a great company and makes a good income. She and her husband divorced when their son was five. She raised him on her own, with no financial support from her ex. Her son recently graduated from college and is teaching English abroad on a fellowship. About 10 years ago, I asked her, "Do you want a new partner?" Her response, "When I finish my bachelor's degree." After her graduation, I asked, "Is it time now?" She said that she had to lose weight. Having lost the weight, "Now?" I asked. "Well, I'm just in the process of applying to graduate school." She has been operating from a belief that she has to accomplish her idea of perfection before she is good enough to attract a partner. Sherry simply doesn't understand what makes a person attractive.

I hear it often: "I'll be attractive when I … lose 20 pounds, get a promotion, or a new car, or…" If you don't see yourself as attractive as you would like, you've probably been short-changed by looking in the wrong mirror – one that's been polished by Mother Culture in which you compare yourself to standards of beauty and success that are either unachievable or somewhere off in the future. Admittedly, while good looks and money are undoubtedly strong magnets, plenty of extremely attractive people possess neither. The tabloids constantly remind us that wealth or physical beauty alone are insufficient to create an enduring intimacy. It's not about the wrapping, but what's inside.

You can be attractive right now by changing the mirror.

A Different Mirror

Put aside the *beauty* mirror for a moment and check out the *inner treasure* mirror. This mirror reflects your attractiveness from the inside out. It shows your appreciation of life. Gazing into this mirror, you can see yourself within an enormous, continuously unfolding, mysterious world, full of hidden gifts. How you feel about yourself and this world radiates your aliveness. Your openness to discovery, your desire to contribute, your gratitude, and self-confidence glows from your core and draws people to your light.

The bad news about this mirror is that it can be harsh when it reveals our human-beingness – our resentment, doubt, and stubbornness. The good news is – this mirror reveals both our abilities and limitations. If you can dream of a different image than the one you see, if you can say, "I want to be..." or "I want to have..." and are committed to make it so, the mirror will reveal the learning you must take on in order to be satisfied with your life.

Appreciating how little we know creates an energy of wonder and a hunger for teachers. Knowing we can learn anything that we put our mind to, confidence expands in short order, as soon as learning begins. Seeing yourself as an unfolding being, finding gratitude for the gifts you have already received and for life itself, taking on the challenges you have been presented with, makes you a treasure hunter, a co-creator with life, who projects the message, "You want to dance with me, because I am a joy to be with." This kind of attractiveness can be generated at any age or stage of life.

So, how attractive are you?

The 10-Test

To get an authentic reflection of your attractiveness, take a balanced look at your satisfaction with where you are in your life. Answer this question honestly, "On a scale of 1-10, 10 being fully satisfied in each of the following areas, what's your number?"

Ten does not mean, "I have achieved perfection," but rather, "I believe that I am in a good place at this point in time and I am moving towards my goal." Because life is a constant unfolding for which you never fully arrive, 10 is not about mastery or even achieving your goals. You could be confined to a wheelchair, unemployed, and with asthma, and still be a 10. Ten is not about anyone else's standards but your own. Ten says, "I am doing the best I can with what I've been given and am working diligently at mining my opportunities."

Each of these domains is critical to well-rounded adulthood:

Body – Am I in as good a shape as I would like to be?

Work – Am I doing fulfilling work for which I am rewarded appropriately?

Finance – Am I comfortable with my money and am I prepared for the future?

Play – Do I have a decent work/life balance?

Family – Do I have functional family relationships in which love trumps difference?

Friends – Do I feel loved and supported by a strong network of friends?

Community – Do I participate in activities of caring for the people amongst whom I live?

Emotion – Am I strong enough to handle breakdowns and disappointments and can I empathize with other's challenges?

Spirituality – Am I at peace with the fact that life is beyond my control and that I will die?

Gratitude – Do I give thanks for the life I've been given?

Any score under 10 in any domain prompts the question, "What is missing in order for you to be satisfied?"

By embracing the learning, a humble, self-confidence begins to ooze. But while learning is something we all have to do and have done, few of us have learned how to embrace it.

Producing Confidence

Confidence is a function of knowing what you know, what you don't know, and recognizing that there will always be a universe of knowledge you are blind to – that which you don't even know that you don't know. You create a mood of wonder when you are open and appreciate discovering things you had no idea about.

To be confident, you don't have to be a master of everything. Confidence comes with being comfortable with your level of competence or incompetence and determining the areas you are committed to build. Your attractiveness becomes substantially diminished any time you think you should know something and fake that you do.

Pretending is an aspect of the "looking-good syndrome" and a major obstacle to taking the first step of learning. Unfortunately, we have been raised in a culture in which knowing equals looking good. We will often go out of our way to pretend that we know when we don't. My friend Peter laughs when he acknowledges that he's so addicted to looking good that he tries to impress the maître d' in any restaurant. In a world in which we have to know, we feel shame at our incompetence. To whatever extent we pretend to be more competent than we are, we suffer. And we look bad.

Here is a tool for confidence-building. It's a scale that will allow you to see your current level of competence and shape your expectations for learning:

Producing Openness and Wonder

We are generally vague when we speak about our competence. *I know this* or *I'm pretty good at that*. We don't like to think of ourselves as *incompetent*. But in reality, we are all operating at some level of incompetence. It turns out that recognizing the extent of our competence/incompetence is a major factor in confidence building. The Scale of Competence ("The Scale") below is based on the Dreyfus Model of Skill Acquisition, introduced at the University of California, Berkeley in 1980.

The Scale of Competence allows you to see where you are, based on your capacity to take effective action – that is, what you can do versus what you know about, and how flawlessly you execute. According to the neurobiologist Humberto Maturana, knowledge equals action. Information only signifies awareness for someone who hasn't yet entered the game. I know a lot about the game of golf – the rules and tools, etc., because I've watched it on TV. But I couldn't hit better than 120 on 18 holes.

Psychologists David Dunning and Justin Kruger have done extensive studies to demonstrate that people with low levels of competence suffer from illusory superiority – they think they're much more capable than they are.[1] This cognitive bias impedes their ability to recognize their own ineptitude and evaluate their competence accurately. And it makes them look like buffoons. It's curious that there seems to be a cultural aspect to this phenomenon. Americans are more likely to have this bias than Asians, for example. Authentic confidence is available at any level. A confident beginner says, "I'm making mistakes but I'm learning, and I love it."

Here is an overview of eight stages of competence, applicable in every domain of life. I will further clarify them in the following pages.

1. Blind – a bull in the china shop, you don't even know that you don't know

2. Pre-beginner (or not in the game) – you are aware of the domain but incapable of taking effective action

3. Beginner – you are just learning the basics, work with a coach

---

1 Unskilled and Unaware of it: How Difficulties in Recognizing One's Own Incompetence Lead to Inflated Self-Assessments, *Journal of Personality and Social Psychology*, 1999

4. Minimally competent – you are capable of taking unsupervised basic actions without getting into trouble

5. Competent – you can deal with multiple activities, make plans, and develop routines

6. Proficient – you can perceive deviations from the normal pattern, employ maxims for guidance

7. Virtuoso – you are a world class performer, transcend reliance on the rules, and have an intuitive grasp on situations

8. Master – you are someone who invents a whole new game

The development of moral agency is linked with the advancement of expertise. Basically, the more competent you are, (competent in the sense of capacity to take action rather than simply having information), the better your decision-making. It seems obvious that this is the case, but what is new here?

As we develop competence and begin to learn from our mistakes, we often look back at the past with the belief that we could have operated more competently. But, in fact, most likely, it just wasn't possible. The failures that source our regret come down to having made a choice between doing what was hard or what was easy at the time.

From a linguistic perspective, *hard* and *easy* are not descriptors of activity. Rather they describe the actor's competence. Juggling five balls at a time, for example, may look hard if you are not competent, but juggling is easy for someone who has learned how. The choices we make are based on our competence to act. These are the only actions we are capable of taking. The real failure is not understanding that no matter how bad the choice, you were still doing the best you could with the competence you had at the time.

BLIND

We can't be any more incompetent than to be blind. Blindness is an unavoidable human condition. Cognitive blindness – being in a space of not knowing that you don't know or what we don't know – affects us all. We will always live amidst vast areas of blindness, even if we are in school 24 hours a day for the rest of our lives. Accepting your blindness makes for curiosity and openness to discovering the world. We are all blind and are greatly benefitted by others who can show us.

Do you know about *watsu*? No? Did you ever hear of it? No? That's what blindness feels like. (Watsu, by the way, is a type of Japanese water massage.)

Now that you know about watsu, you've officially moved up The Scale to become a **PRE-BEGINNER**.

PRE-BEGINNER

You're aware of the domain but not yet in the game because you're unable to take effective action. As a pre-beginner, you can get a watsu massage but you ought not try to give one. A pre-beginner can choose to learn or not. After all, we can't be competent at everything. But there are some domains in life that we can't avoid learning if we want to be autonomous adults – money, health, for instance.

BEGINNER

If you're committed to learn watsu, cooking, Excel, or anything else, you can seek a course of learning, and move up The Scale to become a **BEGINNER**. Learning anything that's complex, playing the violin, for example, will require more than a book to get competent. You'll need a coach, someone with the ability to show you what you can't see.

After struggling with writing this book for a couple

of years, I'd amassed several hundred pages but no book. Cristián asked me if I was committed to complete it. I assured him I was. Then he asked me to assess my competence to write a book. I told him that I was obviously a beginner as I had never written a book before. "And who," he asked, "is your coach?" I didn't have one. Blindness strikes again. Within a couple of months in working with a coach, I produced a proposal and engaged an agent. That was a good start, but eight weeks is hardly enough to produce real competence. A proposal is one thing; a book is another. There was still much for me to learn.

Coaches Drive Competence

Anyone with a commitment to master anything – think Pavarotti, Rafael Nadal, or anyone in professional performance – hungers to discover areas of blindness that will improve their game. People pay big money to coaches who can show them what they're blind to and invite their criticism rather than balk at it.

Coaches are more than occasional advisors. They schedule regular time for reflection and establish practice plans that will ensure the achievement of new levels of competence. They inspire learning by revealing the gap between where you are and the next level of competence. They provide new distinctions, help define positive outcomes, and support you in valuing the discomfort of falling and failing, demanding you never speak poorly of yourself in the face of a shortfall.

Coaches highlight what you have done well or poorly, strengthen your capacity to self-observe, and support you in managing your mood. Confidence grows as you witness your own learning and move up The Scale.

MINIMALLY COMPETENT/COMPETENT/ PROFICIENT

Each level of The Scale is associated with specific action, from the basics to the ability to teach others. A beginner works for some time to be able to take action without supervision. More time and practice is necessary to become competent. More time still for proficiency.

In sharing this Scale of Competence with my younger daughter's fiancé, a Cordon-Bleu-trained chef, I asked him to tell me the actions that a competent chef could execute. Because competent people can speak easily about what they do, rather than say, "cook a good meal," he easily rattled off various activities – vegetable preparation (concassé tomatoes), knife skills (slicing an onion to a 16th" dice), appropriating cookware, timing skills that would allow all components to be ready at the peak of flavor. Listening to him was a mouth-watering experience.

Switching domains – because competence in one domain does not signify competence in another – I asked him if he could tell me the actions of a competent husband. Imagine the response of someone who had never been married nor was raised by loving, connected parents.

He stumbled around looking for answers but, "Um" and "trust" were his best utterances. Obviously, being a proficient chef does not make for a proficient husband. Until that moment, he had been *blind* to marriage as a domain of competence and was about to do what so many of us have done – fall in love and get married. (They never did.)

No one is a proficient person. Levels of competence vary by domain.

VIRTUOSO/MASTER

Learning takes time. In 2011, Malcolm Gladwell, in his book Outliers: The Story of Success, said that aspiring to mastery requires a commitment to approximately 10,000 hours. That comes to about three hours every day for 10 years. That's the amount of time Bill Bradley said he dedicated to become a New York Knick and a US Senator in his book We Can All Do Better (2012).

You can use this scale to assess every activity in every domain of life – body, money, sports, family, community, and so forth. Competence is measured by action.

When you look at yourself through the lens of The Scale, it becomes obvious that masters are rare – think Einstein, Alexander Bell, Edison, Galileo, Darwin, Jobs. Virtuosos are few and far between. You are likely to be competent in a couple of domains, perhaps proficient in one or two, and in many others, a beginner or not in the game. Accepting this reality with no pretense for being more competent than you are, with a commitment to learn, creates openness.

Declaring your commitment and working with a coach, and operating with a sense of wonder, you can joyfully define your goals and produce a roadmap to arrive at your destination.

Confidence is the result of feeling satisfied that you're on track. You are connected to the right people, you see possibilities for the future, you're doing a decent job of what's important, and grateful to life. If you are committed to establish an attractive identity – the key is to become a great learner.

What's an Identity?

Your identity is not simply a function of what you think about yourself. I began to understand this at 19, when I was fired from one of my first jobs as an administrative assistant at a collection agency. I had no real skills. All I had to do was answer phones and send out letters and payment demands. While I was cleaning out my desk, I resentfully thought, "If only these people could know who I really am," as if my identity were held in some secret compartment deep inside me that they might discover. For my bosses, I was casual in my work, a tad sloppy, often late, ignored direction, and did things my way. In short, a teenager. Meanwhile, I thought of myself as smart, cute, and sassy. My mother's voice echoed, "Who do you think you are?"

Over the years, I discovered that "who I am" is not simply a matter of self-perceived qualities. Identity lives in the stories that go on around us. People talk about you in terms of:

- How you are seen in the world

- Who you love and are connected to

- Your ethics – what you value and stand for and how consistently you live those values

- How you have dealt with the bad things that have happened in your life – how well you have restored dignity and appreciation in your life

When there is coherence between what you think about yourself and the way the world sees you, there's no pretense and you have greater resonance with others.

Don't get stuck in the idea that at this age, you should have already learned thus and such. Well, you can say that you should have, but it is not an accurate representation of what would have been possible at the time. You learn only when you recognize the need. Now is exactly the right time.

Accepting that learners make mistakes means you can attribute your failures to incompetence rather than insuffi-ciency. If you've produced some damage, you can apologize with dignity, commit to learning, ask forgiveness, and move on, without shame or regret. With a serious commitment to learn from your mistakes, when "I should have…" crosses your mind or your lips, you might say instead, "Alas, I wish I could have, but I was a bozo then and have learned a strong lesson since." Compassion comes easily for those who accept their beginnerhood.

The key to shifting out of regret and shame is embracing failure as part of life's ever-present demand for learning. Rather than judging ourselves as good or bad people with certain character flaws, our salvation lies in becoming learners who can rigorously assess our competence and determine where we are committed to building it. No one gets to be an expert person in the totality of their life. While you may be an expert chef, you may, at the same time, be a beginner at tennis, public speaking, or parenting.

Confidence builds as you define what you have to learn and set about the learning. You don't have to be more competent to be satisfied. You can appreciate the journey. Confidence is a light that shines from within that reflects your knowing that you're learning and that life is working.

Journal:

The purpose of this journal is to increase your sense of attractiveness by focusing your attention on the identity you have, the one you want to create, and clarifying the learning necessary to produce it. The questions may be confronting, but your answers will pave the path to confidence, openness, and wonder.

1. Are you someone who radiates confidence and openness?

2. What is your identity? Write four paragraphs, one each, that describes:

    a. The important relationships in your life

    b. How you contribute – what you do and how well you do it

    c. The values you stand for

    d. How you have mined the difficulties you've had to face in your life

3. Are you satisfied with that description? Do you want to be known differently?

4. What do you want to have that you don't have now?

5. Consider your own level of competence according to the Scale of Competence in the following domains. Are you a beginner? Do you have a coach? If you are competent or higher on The Scale, detail the actions that you can perform.

    a. Relationship

    b. Career

    c. Parenting

    d. Money

    e. Body

    f. Hobbies (sports)

    g. Community

    h. Spirituality

6. What do you want to be able to do that you can't do now?

7. Are there situations in which you are inclined to pretend that you know more than you actually do?

8. What are you committed to learn?

9. To whom can you talk about finding a coach?

10. Will you commit to getting a coach? And by when?

11. How do you feel about your attractiveness now?

12. What fears or anxieties do you have about moving forward?

KEY TWO

Learn the Basic Moves

"A human being becomes whole not in virtue of a relation to himself [only] but rather in virtue of an authentic relation to another human being."

—Martin Buber

THE DANCE OF relationship has been going on since the time before time. The dance is like the Big Dipper – always present but invisible – until it is pointed out to you. Seeing it for the first time is as powerful an experience as first seeing the Earth from space. It puts life in a different perspective.

The dance takes place in language. Every time you speak, you are performing a move. To begin to see the dance, focus on your interactions with others, at home and at work, to get things done and plan the future. Some interactions are short and simple, like ordering a latte at Starbucks. Some are extended and complex, like building a house or organizing a party. Every dance presents an opportunity to be satisfied.

Or not. When you pay attention to how you enroll others to coordinate with you, you'll see that when you're enrolling, you're leading the dance. When you are asked for something, you're following.

You, as well as everyone you know, are performing the same dance moves, over and over. To be graceful and connected you must learn how to execute them intentionally. The good news is there are only six basic moves to learn to create a career, relationship, intimacy, and community. When you and your dance partners know the moves and can execute them competently, you glide through life. Learning to lead and follow this invisible dance may well be one of the most important educations of your life.

The repetitive patterns in the dance of relationship were first identified by two linguist/philosophers named John Searle and J. L. Austin in the 1950-60's. In researching the way people establish their connections, coordinate actions, and navigate the world in language, they distinguished a dynamic structure they called, "Speech Act Theory"[2]. They showed that with only a few basic moves, we are able to understand our environment and each other, define what we want and need, and take action with others to manifest our visions. With these same six moves, we intend to:

1. Declare – establish new entities, policies, or set direction,

2. Assert– determine the truth, state verifiable facts,

3. Assess – present our opinions, feelings, and values,

4. Request – ask someone to take action,

5. Offer – propose to take action for others, and

6. Promise – commit to do or deliver something in the future.

2 *How to Do Things with Words, The William James Lectures Delivered at Harvard University in 1955,* Oxford Clarendon Press, 1962

If you are going to be graceful in the dance of relationship, it's essential to remember these six moves. Here's my favorite acronym:

O-ffer

P-romise

R-equest

A-ssertion

D-eclaration

A-ssessment!

OPRADA!

Here's an example of the six moves in action – a stereotypical after-work family conversation:

She: Hello (**Declaration** of greeting – I see you). How was your day (**Request** for information)?

He: Good… long (**Assessment**). I closed that deal with Johnson (**Assertion**). I'm so glad to be home (**Declaration** of gratitude).

She: You said you were coming home early (**Assertion** implying a complaint which is an **Assessment**). I wanted you to take Jake to the football game in 15 minutes (A **request** that may have been clear in the past, or not).

He: No, I didn't say that (Conflicting **Assertion** – either it's true or he's lying). Jeez, I haven't eaten (**Assertion** and another implied complaint – **Assessment** – you shouldn't be asking).

She: Never mind (**Cancel request**). I'll do it (**Promise**). Dinner is in the oven (**Assertion**). I will be back by nine (**Promise**) and we can watch the game together (**Offer**).

You can't do anything other than these six moves. We are making them all the time, over and over, in various combinations. The content changes but the moves are constant.

The misalignment in the conversation left both partners irritated. As so often happens in the dance, one partner says something and the other hears it differently than was intended. That's because speaking and hearing are two different functions, shaped by each person's unique history. When you accept this reality, you avoid a "You said/No I didn't" battle, which always ends in lose/lose. You give up blaming conversations like, "But you said" or "I was perfectly clear." The only option in the face of miscoordination, and it's a really dignified one, is to say, "What I understood was…" It honors your partner.

If he honestly believed that he didn't say he'd be home early, and she believed he did, the way to restore balance and alignment might sound something like this:

She: Didn't you say you were coming home early (**Request**)? That's what I based my planning on (**Assertion**).

He: I meant I would be home at a reasonable hour (**Assertion**). If you had told me about the game, I could have been home an hour ago (**Assessment**).

She: I don't know why, after all these years, you can't read my mind (**Assessment** – intended as humor).

Taking Responsibility Shifts the Mood

Knowing about the moves may be interesting. Unaware of them, it's hard to know what you're doing when you open your mouth. Or what others are doing. Because language can be very confusing, we've got to get underneath the words to the intentions. For example, if someone says, "I suggest you work over the weekend," you need to know if the speaker intended to request that you work or share an assessment. Without knowing the moves and clarity on the intention, you'll make plans based on your own way of speaking. The rank of the speaker is also likely to be an influence. It takes focus to ensure you're aligned with the speaker's intention. To clarify, you might ask, "Are you asking me to work this weekend or do you think that it would be a good idea?"

When you put aside the idea that 'love is a feeling that happens to me' and embrace love as 'the feeling I create in my dance with others,' you can see that by declaring "I love you," you bring into being your deep appreciation and gratitude for the other in your life. You create a space of tenderness and devotion. A great dance partner fosters appreciation. More satisfaction, more gratitude, more love (and more sex, if you're interested).

By declaring, you take a stand about the importance of others to you, not just about what they do for you. When you hear, "I love you," and know what those three words mean to the speaker, you feel valued.

What follows is a brief overview of the moves. They are the foundation for every step of the dance. I will go more deeply into how to make them effectively in each of the subsequent chapters.

The Dance in Six Moves (the overview)

Since the dance of relationship is going on all the time transparently, as long as you're feeling good about how life is flowing, you can mindlessly be in the moment and go with the flow. Feelings of uneasiness or dissatisfaction, however, are signals that it's time to focus on the dance. You take the lead when you assume responsibility for improving a difficult situation.

The key to a better future is listening, simply paying attention – to the world, to your heart's desire and wisdom, and to others. Robert Frost says that virtuosity in listening "is the ability to listen to almost anything without losing your temper or your self-confidence." Knowing the moves is the path to virtuosity.

Listening to the World
Asserting and Assessing

Before you dance, you want to have a sense of the space – where the pillars are located on the dance floor, the number of other dancers around whom you must navigate, the tempo of the music – what is fixed and what is changeable. In the dance of life, you attune to the world around you with two moves – asserting and assessing.

Asserting – Stating the Facts

We assert what is true, witnessable, and unchangeable. Assertions describe the indisputable circumstances about what has happened in the past or what is happening now. The future, which is unpredictable, can only be assessed. After all, while there are tremendous odds in favor of the sun rising and setting at certain times, we have to recognize that odds are assessments. And odds are beaten regularly.

The nature of assertions is that they are cut and dried, neither good nor bad. I was 19 when I married and 25 when I divorced. Those are the facts. My feelings about them, my assessments, make them positive or negative.

"It's 48 degrees outside," is an assertion. It can be verified by the thermometer. "It's cold," is an assessment.

"I'm a manager" is an assertion. It's the job title. "I manage people" is an assessment because "managing" is a general term which cannot be measured or verified. "I have conducted weekly staff meetings every Monday for the past year" is also an assertion.

Assertions present THE truth in the world – undeniable,

facts. Assessments present MY truth – my honest perception about the world. And these two truths are often confused.

Assessing – Speaking Your Mind

Good and bad, valuable and worthless, hot and cold, neat and sloppy, competent and incompetent – all assessments, all opinions or judgments. They aren't right or wrong. They're personal. A 48-degree day may be warm for an Alaskan and frigid to a Colombian. Both assessments are valid and neither is right.

Assessments about the future can only be deemed right or wrong after the fact. If, in 2015, you predicted (assessed) that Donald Trump would be elected President of the United States, we could only assert that you were right after election day.

Beliefs are assessments that are held as facts. They open up a whole new can of worms. Is there a heaven? Did man evolve from apes? People with answers to those questions are fervent. The 'shoulds' fall into the same category. Should you starve a fever and feed a cold? Is a college degree a must? Those who would try to convince you that you should behave in a certain way and insist that they are right, produce imbalance and upset in the dance.

You assess what's possible and your best options. You're assessing when you speculate about the future. To start a serious process of speculation, bring in other people you trust, a caring and competent network of support, to help you see what you can't see and challenge your thinking.

Some assessments, while they are not true, can be extraordinarily useful. The capacity to make well-grounded assessments, opinions that won't float away like a lot of hot air, is a critical skill. The essential elements include specifics as to why you say what you say, the background of assertions that support your view, and clarity about the standards of measurement.

For example, to ground the assessment that Greenhill (or XYZ) School is the best choice for your kids, I could state, "They are a college prep school since 1950, and last year, 92% of graduates were accepted into four-year colleges." This assessment may be useful to anyone who shares my concerns, but for someone interested in a more arts-oriented or vocational school, this assessment may not be as useful. Knowing more about why people say what they say creates a clearer path to the future.

There's a lot more to say about assessments and how to make them effectively. I will go into further detail as we explore telling the hard truth and conflict. But for now, once you're clear about where you want to go, let's focus on the move that sparks action – declaration.

Declaring The Move that Initiates Action

Declaring is an act of creation. "I love you" is a declaration. It is a stand that I take, the foundation for all of my actions surrounding my relationship with you. With a declaration, you move from wanting, hoping, dreaming, aspiring, and conspiring into action. In the act of declaring, you define the dream you're committed to bring into reality and establish the conditions under which you will be satisfied.

Declaring a vision with the force of, "Come hell or high water, I'm going to get that!" provides the context for life – a commitment to motherhood, with or without a partner, for example.

There are some circumstances in which change is impossible. In those cases, the only option is to accept the way it is and declare, "There's nothing I can do (or want to do). I'm in peace." You may not like it, but you can accept it as part of life.

Death, for instance. You can both dislike it (assess) and accept it (declare) simultaneously. While grief is a natural response to loss, it is a powerful process that must be experienced. At the same time, it is possible to live with grief in peace and joy. The amount of time it takes to release the physical and psychic bonds of our interconnectedness varies greatly. Acceptance of the fragile nature of life eases the transition.

You create alliances with declarations. Family is biological. Relationships beyond blood are established by declaration. You get to say who is your friend or your partner. With declarations, you institute boundaries, rules of the road, and consequences for not following the rules.

Standards of excellence are declared. An important question must be brought forth: Who has the authority to declare or change standards? You can declare for yourself but for no one else, other than a minor child in your custody. Similarly, no one can make declarations for you unless you grant them authority. "I pronounce you married (or divorced)" creates a new reality if it is said by a judge. "Office hours are 9-5." "Women must wear hose and may not wear sleeveless blouses." If you don't like the rules or standards established by the powers that be, you can declare, "I quit." Or you can declare, "This must change," and move into action to produce it.

Asserting what's fixed and assessing what's changeable establishes the ground on which you can build the future. Declarations provide impetus for your action and they begin to shape your identity. Declaring your commitment, you are propelled into the next part of the dance – the dance of action.

The Dance of Action
Requesting, Offering, and Promising

Action is a dance of change that will produce satisfaction and money, build identity, and grow intimacy. Being clear about what you want to change, you can **request** someone do something for you, or you can **offer** to do something for someone else. You can make requests or offers to anyone, as long as they are receptive. How do you know if they're open? You ask them.

Requesting

It's a pleasure to ask for something and get exactly what you wanted. And sometimes, you get more than what you expected and it's incredible. You are more likely to get what you want when you are specific about what it is that you want, when you want it, and ask someone who is capable of making it happen. Simple? Yes! Easy? Sure, after you practice.

As the requestor, you lead the dance. The first rule is: Don't ask someone to do something who's not open to your requests. That might seem obvious, but sometimes we disturb people who are focused on other things. In leading an action dance, it's important to engage partners who are happy to dance with you. Pressuring people to do something will often backfire. They may accede to your request, but the dance will be less than satisfying.

When you find someone competent who wants to dance, be as clear as possible about what you want. Specificity isn't easy for some people (women particularly), often because they come from a background where specific=direct=pushy. Making requests that are clear *and* gentle is something that can be learned.

You honor your partners when you ensure that they know they can decline your requests. You have to make room for a 'no.' This is new thinking for a lot of people because, somehow, we have conflated decline with rejection and believe, "If you loved me, you would…" This kind of pressure denies another's legitimacy and is an act of aggression. A decline is a declaration that simply says, "I'm not open to that. I love you, respect you, and am happy to receive your requests in the future."

Anyone who can't say "no" is probably in the army, listening to a commanding officer. Commands are still requests. They just carry a higher consequence for declining. Can your kids decline? Can your lover? Do people salute you?

In the face of decline or push back, don't try to convince others that they ought to, or guilt them into doing what you're asking. Requests do not need to be justified. Your reasons may be motivating, or not. The best you can ask for from someone who declines is a willingness to explore other ideas for addressing your concerns.

"Please clean your room" may be the most ignored request in recorded time. If that's an issue for you, here are some questions for reflection: Is your kid open to your request? If not, why not? ("Because they're teenagers" isn't a good enough answer.) Do they share the same standards of "clean?" Are there policies in place that have been bought into? Are you clear about timing? Are you asking for and getting a promise? Are there consequences for non-fulfillment?

The dance of action moves forward when the listener and speaker are aligned and they promise – the listener to deliver, and you, the speaker, to be satisfied when the conditions are fulfilled. Then you're rolling.

Offering

Offering is another way to get what you want. Propose to do something for someone else because it serves you to serve them – either for the joy of it or for some exchange. It is a way to show people they are valued. At the same time, your offers are the basis for your work in the world and your identity.

Find a need and offer to fill it. If you want change in your world, make an offer to someone who will benefit from the change. Rather than asking someone to do something for you, offers can have you appear as an answer to someone's prayers. "Here's what I can do for you" is the basis for your reputation.

Offering is simple but, again, not so easy. Good offers include the same basic elements as good requests: clear conditions of satisfaction that you will provide, as well as what you want in exchange, even if you're doing it just for the pleasure. "I'd love to cook you dinner tonight. How does lasagna sound? Would you bring some red wine around 7?"

Don't take offense at a decline. If your offer isn't inviting, either change your offer or find someone else to offer it to. Perhaps you can negotiate – make a counteroffer – adjust your conditions of satisfaction.

And just like requests, no action should take place until the offer is accepted.

Promising – the Move that Creates the Future

To promise is to say, "You can count on me." Rather than a moral obligation, promising is the way we invent the future. Because it's always now, a week from Tuesday only exists in our speaking and listening and on our calendars.

How consistently and reliably you fulfill your promises is the basis for a trustworthy identity. It is possible to maintain trust even in the times that life gets in the way of your best intentions when you responsibly manage your lack of fulfillment. That means – being in communication as soon as you know you won't be able to fulfill and taking care of any consequences of the broken commitment. For example, if I promised you a ride to the airport on Sunday but was requested on Friday to work the weekend, a trust-building move would be to call as soon as I discovered that I couldn't fulfill and explore how else you could get there. If it's really a problem for you, I could offer to pay for a cab.

Promising and commitment management are some of the most important relationship agreements. This is a big area of blindness for many couples and families. It is critical to establish ground rules for count-on-ability and how breakdowns will be handled should they occur.

Once a promise is made, the activities of fulfillment begin. Complex action dances, projects for work, your house, or your kid's school, for example, take time to complete and usually require the commitments of others involved in the process. Everybody engaged in a project must be clear about the milestones along the way and that their promises are being counted on.

You don't have to wait for completion to be satisfied. While you might be eager for the end result, patience is possible when you accurately assess how much time something will take and meet your interim goals. And patience is fertile ground for gratitude.

The dance of action is over when someone declares, "It's complete." If you are satisfied, declare it. "Thank you" is a declaration that you appreciate the other's efforts, but it doesn't equate to, "I'm satisfied." Authentic declarations of gratitude strengthen the bonds of relationship. So does saying, "I'm not satisfied," if you say it with honor not anger. Understanding the source of the breakdown will help you decide if you want to begin a new dance of action. In the face of failure or an unsatisfactory result, gratitude is still possible when you discover something important.

Toe-mashing
(or what happens when the moves are confused)

We only discover a lack of shared understanding when the dance breaks down. We thought things were clear because we asked, "Do you understand?" We so often fail because we assume that others who speak the same language understand our words. Even in English-speaking countries, the meaning of "yes" varies from "definitely" to "I'll try." We clarify by adding, "Can I count on you?"

Beware of your assumptions. What seems obvious to you is never worth mentioning. My husband and his siblings had been planning an 80th birthday celebration for his father for months. Cristián purchased plane tickets, a venue was selected, and menus were established. No one, however, had thought to talk to his father about the planning until one month before the event. That's when they discovered that his father had made other plans to celebrate out of town with his partner. They were flabbergasted. "How could this be?" His father never missed a family birthday celebration. No shared background of obviousness can definitely screw up your dance.

When I said, "Come for dinner at 7pm," I didn't say "7 sharp," because it was obvious to me that 7 meant 7. When they showed up closer to 8pm and the lasagna was fairly dried out, I was triggered to be annoyed. Breakdowns always reveal bad assumptions. It was then clear that coming from a different culture, they didn't share the same background of obviousness – another example of speaking/listening disparity. The expectation of alignment is as crazy as speaking English to a Martian and counting on seamless synchronization. My bad! Taking responsibility for attunement, I could easily see what was missing – a lack of shared understanding about what we each meant, wanted, and needed. I would have been better able to coordinate our dance had I asked, "Can you be there by 7 sharp?"

Toes will be mashed when you aren't clear about your request. Making an assessment like, "It's cold in here," usually doesn't work well. My mother would do that. I once asked her why she didn't just ask for what she wanted. She replied, "I don't like to have to ask for things." She is not alone in this way of thinking. You must specify your request if you expect something to happen – you would like a sweater, a blanket, or the heat turned up.

Toes will be mashed when you assume that others' requests are declarations. In every relationship, you must know if you have room to decline or counteroffer. And you do a great service to others by letting them know they have that space. It's a way to demonstrate honor. This doesn't mean that people don't have to do their job or what they promised. Rather it gives them freedom to express when they are challenged.

One of the greatest sources of damage to a relationship is the battle for "who's right." Believing your assessment is THE truth and insisting that you are right will jettison you into protracted debate. Our need to be right is treacherous to relationship. Think about the amount of time you have spent in your life debating assessments. We are so quick to disagree with another's opinion that we often shut down our willingness to listen or walk away from the conversation.

Your ability to distinguish between assertions and assessments gives you tremendous power to produce alignment. Simply asking "Is that a fact or an opinion?" can produce a necessary pause for reflection.

When you are clear that multiple interpretations of any situation are always possible, it becomes easier to validate others for their different opinions and point of view. Rather than disagreeing with a contrary opinion, a better move is to seek to understand where the other is coming from. Try instead, "Really? I'm curious about why you would say that. Tell me more." This move opens the channels of relatedness. Being clear that there is no definitive proof for a belief and that multiple valid assessments can co-exist, you can say, "I have a different opinion," and give up debating forever.

You show respect when you temporarily set aside your own assessments to examine the possibilities that a different point of view may offer. This can only happen when you don't have to defend yourself or insist that you are right – about the way things are, why they are that way, or the possibilities you see around you.

Taking responsibility for the quality of your dance with others and being mindful of the moves and how effectively you are making or have made them is the basis for a most joyful existence. Any time life doesn't appear to be working, your choices are to accept the failure in peace, as part of life beyond your control, view it as a call for learning… or you can suffer, stuck in that physical, emotional, spiritual pain that is produced by the self-talk, "It shouldn't be this way." Suffering will continue as long as the "should" stays in place.

Life is amazing when partners understand the moves they are making and are committed to constantly improving their moves. Breakdowns, while they can be greatly reduced through practice with the moves, will never be completely eradicated because two different people will always have breakdowns in obviousness. The best we can do is appreciate that blindness is an unavoidable part of life and forgive ourselves for our inability to see what's often right in front of us.

Journal:

Simply knowing *about* the moves does not make you competent to execute them. To dance in relationship effectively, you must have the ability to pay attention to how you are being and moving in the world, in the moment. Improvement comes rapidly when you make time for self-reflection. Regularly asking the following questions, "What am I focusing on right now? Am I satisfied? What am I committed to? What moves have I made and can I plan to create change?" builds a mindful observer with greater ease in the dance of relationship. As you practice observing your thoughts and actions, you activate a higher level of your consciousness.

The journal provides a daily practice for dancing with grace. The greater your capacity to reflect on what is happening in the moment, the easier it is to attune and reattune. Your journal works similarly to a video that performance professionals use to review how they did. You assess what worked and what didn't, and prepare to focus your practice. The journal's critical questions and practical exercises are structured to help you define your vision of a meaningful and successful life, and determine the next actions for how you can live it. By setting aside a few minutes each day to journal, you will immediately begin to build a greater capacity for love.

1. Did I get everything I wanted today at work?

   What requests did I make today?

   Did I specify my conditions of satisfaction including time?

   If not, why not?

   Did I grant the freedom to decline or counter-offer my requests?

   Did I receive a promise? Did I ask for one?

   What requests were made to me today?

   Did I have the freedom to decline or counter-offer?

   Were the conditions of satisfaction clear?

   Did I promise?

   What offers did I make today?

   Did we specify shared conditions of satisfaction?

   What disagreements arose today?

   Were they disagreements about assertions or assessments?

   In the face of the disagreement, could I move to curiosity and say, "Tell me more"?

2. Did I get everything I wanted today at home?

   Do you assess a mood of cooperation?

Did you make requests with specific conditions of satisfaction?

Did you get promises?

What do you want that you haven't asked for? Why not?

KEY THREE

Honor Your Partner

*"Humankind has not woven the web
of life. We are but one thread within it.
What we do to the web we do to ourselves.
All things are bound together. All things
connect. We are part of the earth and it is
part of us."*

–Chief Seattle

RACEFUL DANCES BEGIN and end with a bow, a way of honoring your partner. Honor is an attracting energy in the web of life and the foundation of a loving relationship. While it's a commonly used word, honor's meaning is often unclear and not necessarily shared.

What is honor? Fundamentally, to honor is to recognize others as sovereign, worthy of love and non-violence, and with the freedom to decline. As Humberto Maturana and Gerda Verden-Zoller explain in their book *The Origins of Humanness in the Biology of Love,* "Honor is the acceptance of the other as a legitimate other in coexistence with oneself," exactly the way he or she is. Accepting the legitimacy of another means, "I'm not going to try to change you."

Indigenous cultures see a web of life in which everyone and everything is interconnected and interdependent. It's simple to see. Looking deeply into a grain of corn you can see the sun, the rain, the birds, the farmers, and the ancestors who brought the corn to our land from Mexico. Each component is an essential part. Recognizing and appreciating their value is an act of honor.

Namaste, a common greeting in Eastern culture, expresses honor well, "The god in me bows to the god in you." In the film *Avatar,* the Na'vi acknowledged the presence of the other with a simple expression – "I see you." When we are seen, love expands. Relationship deepens as we maintain connection, listen, and understand the other's challenges and accomplishments.

Real honor – consistently valuing all others – is something of a rarity in the Western culture of rugged individualism where "I" is a separate center of awareness. Discreet entities have to figure out life and make it on their own. Westerners prize personal accomplishment and live in a predominant game in which the goal is self-fulfillment. As individuals, we fall into a ranking system based on class, race, income, marital status, and sexual preference, and constantly struggle to be enough.

Not having been raised in a culture that supports honoring all of life all of the time, it comes down to making a choice about how you want to live – to recognize the god in others or not. Honor is a place to come from. I was born in New York City. Where I come from is the belief that we are all one and deserve kindness. Honor is a stand you take – a declaration you make that orients your actions.

How We Honor

Honoring as a conscious choice requires paying attention. Typically, in our self-centered way, we ignore the world around us and take much of life for granted – living in our own bubbles, oblivious of our surroundings. In our unconsciousness, we step on toes and create a domino effect of dishonor. Here's a perfect example of how dishonor expands into the larger community. Standing on line, I was behind a middle aged, black woman who was patiently waiting to purchase some breakfast pastries when a young, white man cut in front of her and said, "I'll have a blueberry muffin." The woman voiced her indignation to the counterman, "Excuse me, I've been waiting here." The server apologized, redirected his attention to her, and asked what she would like. She said, "I'll take ALL of your blueberry muffins."

Now, he may not have intentionally cut her off. I mention race and age here because to honor, we must be keenly aware of our prejudice, biases, and cultural ranking. But failing to honor, either by lack of consciousness or disdain, can come across as aggression and inevitably produces breakdowns in the ease and flow of our dance with others. Pervasive dishonor is destroying our communities.

Honor is simple but not necessarily easy. A gaze of acknowledgment, listening generously, speaking kindly, creating space for another's difference, and expressing gratitude or appreciation are fundamental demonstrations of honor. These actions require practice.

The Gaze of Honor

While our eyes receive information, they also powerfully transmit. In tango, the "mirada" is the way you look in someone's eyes to ascertain if they want to dance with you. In our normal day-to-day existence, we can honor others by simply meeting their eyes.

Honor is a constant challenge when we are face to face with people who trigger our discomfort. For me, confronting the massive homelessness in my city is a daily test. A commitment to honor brought me to volunteer at the Coalition for the Homeless. And still, I am a work of honor in progress, and the work has given me some remarkable experiences.

July 20, 2010, is a date I won't forget. I was waiting for a long overdue subway on a steamy, crowded platform. As I lunged for the only seat on the packed train, I wound up sitting next to an obese, smelly man in a dirty, ripped sweatshirt who was acting very bizarrely – hunched over, head in hands, and mumbling loud nonsense. Disgust was my first reaction. There was no place else to go. I was hemmed in by the crowd and chose to take the situation as another learning opportunity. I knew I needed to change my attitude and find my honor. I began to listen. Trying to understand him, I felt no threat.

When I peeked out of the corner of my left eye to get a better picture of who he was, I saw a large tattoo on his right arm – an eagle, an anchor, and a globe, with a date in the center, 7-21-71. An ex-marine, I thought. I turned to the man and said, "Happy Birthday." He was blown out of his self-absorption and demanded, "How'd you know that?"

I twinkled at him, "I know things." Again, he insisted, "How'd you know that?" I told him, "I get messages." After another moment or two of dancing back and forth in this way, he got it. And he started to laugh. Then I started to laugh, so hard that I cried. Almost instantaneously, the laughter spread to people who were sitting across from us and then began to ripple through half of the subway car. People were laughing who had no idea why.

Scientists call what happened on the subway *congruent change*. It's just another way of saying that we're all connected. One small act of honor expands to all of us.

I don't want to be Pollyanna about this. We must also listen for danger. I had my head in a dark place one evening as I walked into a convenience store. Conscious of my commitment to honor, I held the door for a young man walking behind me. In a flash, he ripped the handbag off my shoulder, took off running, and left me with the broken finger that tried to hold on. I had been paying more attention to my commitment to be of service than to him and how he was. Focusing on him could have changed the outcome. Actually, listening, being present, centered, and balanced could have changed everything.

A perilous situation worked out differently for Angela Montez. When she was robbed at gunpoint at an Indianapolis check-cashing store, she found the presence of mind to talk with the man about God and prayed with him. The thief later turned himself in.

It's all about tuning our listening.

Listening Generously

To listen is to focus our attention and seek to understand. The problem with our everyday listening is we're often half-assed about it. We multi-task, believing we can effectively divide our minds. But many studies, one most notably from Stanford University[3], say we cannot. Listening generously is further complicated by the erroneous belief that people who speak the same language should understand one another. They frequently don't.

It's not just words we need to listen to, we also must listen to body language. Without ensuring that there's alignment between what the speaker intends and what we listen, we could easily misinterpret that a man who is sitting with crossed arms is angry when, in fact, he is cold. Listening is filtered by past experiences, biases, and personal concerns. Sometimes people say 'yes' when they mean 'no' because they are raised that way. It's up to us to listen more deeply than the words.

3 Proceedings of the National Academy of Sciences (2009) Clifford Nass, Eyal Ophir, Anthony Wagner

Still, the greatest barrier to our listening of others might well be our own internal chatter. While another person is speaking, we are busy talking to ourselves about the usefulness of, or interest in, what they are saying. We try to figure out how quickly we can shut them up. As soon as we believe we have the full picture, we cut them off, and say things like, "Get to the point," or "Land the plane." Would we do this to a god?

Generous listening – the conscious intention to listen to the heart of another – is a way to bow. It requires we call ourselves to attention and reduce surrounding distractions. It takes practice to stop the multi-tasking and self-talk.

Try this: With your friend or a child, for two minutes, listen – not just with your ears, but with two eyes and one heart. Watch how you listen. If you catch your mind wandering, call it back to attention, as if the only thing that matters is the speaking of the other. Then, let that person know what you heard, understood, and felt about what they said, and see if you notice something different.

In our workshops, we send people home to practice one act of mindful, generous listening, and ask that they report back what happened on the following day. This simple act is far more powerful than you might think. The results are consistently outstanding, and occasionally humorous. More than one man's wife found his attention so unusual, she wanted to know what trouble he'd gotten himself into.

One young mother shared her experience with her 3-year-old son. "Normally, when I pick him up from daycare I am preoccupied with many different thoughts – dinner, work, and the multitude of concerns of a working mother. Last night, on the way home, I chose to give him my full attention for a few minutes. My son, an only child, had developed the habit of ordering me around as soon as we walked in the door. But last night, when we arrived, he toddled off to his room and played happily by himself until I called him for dinner."

People who show they are listening with openness and caring make us feel safe, supported, and loved. We can create that space of security when we are practiced at turning away from distractions, putting aside our personal agendas, and quieting the immediate defensiveness of our internal voice of protection. The connection between us is dramatically strengthened when we can authentically say, "I understand why you feel that way."

Listening is easy but remembering to do it is the challenge. There are remembering tricks – tie a string around your wrist, put your watch on the other hand, a post-it on your computer screen, or schedule conversations with a specific reminder. More generous listening creates a habit of honor. Naturally, there will always be times when you don't have the time, capacity, or focus to give others. Rather than trying to fake it, ask for another time to sit together in peace. You move with honor when you acknowledge your inability by saying, "I'd like to give you my full attention, but I don't have the time right now. Can we schedule time later?"

You act with dignity when you ask for someone's full attention, like this:

Me (approaching He who is reading a book): Can I talk to you?

He (still focusing on the page): Sure.

Me: I need you to stop reading and listen to me.

He: (still focusing on the book) I'm listening.

Me: No, you're not.

He: Yes, I am.

Me: Well, I need your undivided attention. If now isn't a good time for you, when would be?

He (closing the book): Let's talk now.

Speaking Kindly

We honor others by speaking with reverence and gratitude. It's what you do in the presence of a treasure. It may be easy enough to enact when life goes smoothly but in the midst of conflict, honor often flies out the window. In battle, we use our words like hatchets to cut the other down to our own size (or smaller) and win. Relationship devolves into struggle – everyone for themselves, survival of the fittest.

How do you dare say, "Fuck you! Go to hell," or "You're such a bastard!" to a god? I've said these words and heard them as well. One day it dawned on me that they are not words you say to a treasure. What happened to my treasure? Choosing to honor is a commitment to speak respectfully, not in hostile, sarcastic, or demeaning ways, even in the inevitable face of conflict.

In our earliest days together, it was easy for Cristián to tell me to shut up. That just sent me through the roof. I was horrified by that language. When we discussed it, he asked me earnestly, "What's the problem with that?" In his family, it was a common expression. My own family baggage – the habit of yelling when I got upset – drove him crazy. We blindly bring our history into our dance with others. Understanding how offensive it was to me, he promised not to say those words to me again. Rather than try to shut me up, he takes responsibility by saying, "I can't continue talking with you right now."

From my side, I have given him permission to monitor my decibel level and cease conversation until I can calm myself. Granting him permission was essential. Without it, a reminder that I'm raising my voice could be interpreted as, "Look at what an unstable human being you are" and escalate the conflict.

A commitment to see the god in others amounts to a commitment to stop abusive language. Stop it! But promising not to speak unkindly is not a magic pill for overcoming bad habits. It takes practice and a willingness to be reminded when we lose our way. Overcoming bad habits is not as simple as making a declaration. "Shut up" could easily and automatically fall from Cristián's lips. But if and when it did, I would remind him about his commitment and he would apologize and take it back. Gracefulness is possible when all partners share a commitment to speak kindly.

Appreciation and Gratitude

We all need to know that we make a difference and that our contribution is valued. "Thank you" is an easy acknowledgment of the contribution of others – a gift, something that's been done, or some way of being. In our busy-ness, we take so much for granted and often forget to express our gratitude for the common gifts of life. As a culture, we do a minimalist job at appreciating others' actions. Rarely do we take the time to fully express our appreciation and do it in a way that is really heard. To fully acknowledge another, go beyond, "Thanks." Articulate what you are thanking this person for.

Powerful acknowledgments speak specifically to what the other has done that has touched you and how it has affected you. For some, being acknowledged makes them uncomfortable, but it's important that they get it and appreciate the expression. Acknowledging others and expressing appreciation is attractive as well as contagious.

At a recent family dinner, my 12-year old grandson Luke remarked that I always seem to be talking about how amazing people are. It gave him pause to recognize that he is more inclined to speak about people's insufficiencies. Once he saw the difference and the amount of joy that is available from each perspective, he said he wanted to come from honor – a really bold move amongst six-graders who struggle to feel good about themselves and often one-up their peers.

We honor others when we value their time. When we're unconscious about honoring, we blunder by launching into our agenda when we've walked into an office or called someone on the phone without ever asking, "Do you have time to talk to me right now?" It's a simple and easy way to bow.

Honor extends beyond the human realm. We walk in honor when we pay attention to the world around us. We are strengthened by our appreciation for the natural world. Trebbe Johnson wrote in her *Orion Magazine* article "Uncommon Gratitude" about stopping in front of a lightning-charred cottonwood tree. She tried to imagine the tree in its former formidable presence and how it nurtured and provided shelter for all the animals, birds, and insects. She was moved to celebrate the abundance of the tree's gifts and offered a gift of her own. Collecting bright stones from a nearby wash, she formed a ring around the base of the tree and placed wildflowers in the holes of the trunk.

We hardly stop to smell the roses. How often do we pause to consider the wonder of an artichoke or a simple drink of water? We take water for granted, even as we know that there are droughts in California and people who walk 15 miles a day in parts of Africa to carry water for their family. You can begin to awaken your observer of the world around you simply by pausing for two seconds before you take a drink of water and giving thanks. Authentic appreciation not only reinforces our feelings of connectedness, it has been shown to have physical benefits in boosted immune systems and superior cardiovascular health.[4]

Appreciating the greatness with which we are surrounded in every moment radiates honor and wonder. Each small act – making someone laugh, "seeing" the stranger we pass in the street, holding a door, giving thanks, affects the happiness or suffering of humanity.

4 Lisa Aspinwall, PhD, University of Utah, WebMD, January 11, 2006

Honoring Myself

The conundrum: obviously, if I am going to honor others as myself, I must first honor myself. Without self-honor, honoring others becomes idolatry. Putting others on a pedestal is unworkable for creating mutually satisfying, loving relationships.

Honoring others begins with my own self-acceptance, an enormous challenge in a culture built on beauty, money, and rank. I must accept myself in all the fullness of my humanity. That means – I accept how I look, the situation I was born into, that I have failed and will continue to make mistakes, produce breakdowns, be disappointed at times, and that in order for my life to have value, I must be of service. This is the perfection of life and the perfection of me.

Self-honor comes with clarity about the meaning of our lives – what we stand for, are committed to, and contribute. You don't have to be a perfect person to honor yourself. Or, maybe it's better said: You already are a perfect person. Because life is continually unfolding, you can never be fully formed. From this perspective, all perceived faults and failures are opportunities for learning. We must release the saintly notion of perfection as having achieved mastery in all domains of life.

Self-honor is radiant. Coming from a perspective that life is evolving for everyone, that they too are doing the best they can, the world becomes a better place, more filled with light.

Ask: How much do I honor myself? On a scale of 1-10, 10 being 'absolutely,' what's my number? If it's less than a 10, go back to Key One, reevaluate what part of yourself is less than worthy of honor, and get going on the learning necessary. Do not proceed further in this book if you can't bow to yourself.

Honoring your partner is acknowledging their godliness and their perfection, even when you think they're wrong. The key is to recognize the validity of their perspective and that they are here to learn. It requires that you know that we each create our reality, our love, and desire in language, and how to execute the six moves of the dance.

Journal:

Seeing yourself as part of a weave, who and how you honor defines an important aspect of your meaningful life story.

1. If you are in an intimate relationship now, reflect on your way of listening, speaking, and expressing gratitude.

2. If you are not in an intimate relationship now, but have been in the past, what role did honoring your partner play?

3. Reflect on your family relationships.

    a. Who do you honor?

    b. How do you demonstrate that honor?

    c. Who honors you?

    d. Do you feel dishonored? By whom? What do they do?

    e. Are there patterns of dishonor in your speaking or listening?

4. Reflect on your work relationships.

    a. Who do you honor?

    b. How do you demonstrate that honor?

    c. Who honors you?

    d. Do you feel dishonored? By whom? What do they do?

e. Are there patterns of dishonor in your speaking or listening?

5. Who have you cut off from speaking?

6. Who have you cut down with your speaking?

7. Perform at least one act of intentional listening and note what happened.

8. What reflections do you have on your ability to listen generously?

9. What new declarations and/or promises are you prepared to make to better live a life with honor?

PART TWO

The Choreography

KEY FOUR

Declare Partnership

"Love does not consist in gazing at each other, but in looking outward together in the same direction."

—Antoine de Saint-Exupery

THE STORY IS all too familiar – falling in love, life is light and breezy. The only thing you hunger for is each other. But endorphins only last so long. Eventually the breeze turns to tempest and good times are harder to find.

Partnering "because we love each other" is an insufficient platform for moving from single independence to coupled interdependence. So, if love alone cannot sustain a long-term relationship, why do it?

Because we dream about the future and challenge ourselves to create it.

Good partnerships make us stronger. If you want to build a building, join forces with others you trust to bring something of value to the table. For success in whatever you're building with others, you have to be working off the same blueprint. In building a life, it's the same thing – choose a partner you can count on to bring joy to the table and lighten the load of the daily existence.

What Do You Need to Partner?

Good partners share a sense of purpose and values. Together you co-create the blueprints for the future. To co-create a future, start with yourself. Who do you say you are and where do you want to go? What will you be doing for work, who will you be connected to, where will you live, and what values of life are important? You don't need a grandiose 10-year plan. Goals are important, however. They orient daily life. So are shared values. It's critical to identify your own. And keep in mind that not everyone has the same ideals about a good life. (This is often shocking to people who believe that they have the right values.) Travel, spiritual practice, volunteerism, and social activism are a few values that may not be held dear by others.

Once you have a sketch or an outline of your vision, find someone who loves it. Sharing your dreams is an act of intimacy. With your eye focused on a specific landing spot, you can powerfully navigate into the future.

At the same time, no matter how noble your goal or how committed your partner, you might not wind up where you thought because life is one part 'what you create' and one part 'circumstances beyond your control.' Shit happens. You have to be able to navigate that too. Therefore, building a good life with another requires a greater commitment to the quality of the journey than to the destination because the present moment is all we really have.

It's always now. Life is consecutive moments of now in which the past and future exist only in our speaking. It's now. And it's still now. Joy is only available in the now. I'm not talking about happiness - that fleeting emotion that rides on the back of circumstance – but a physical, intellectual, emotional and spiritual manifestation of appreciation for life itself. Joy is a frequency, a unique vibration of life. You tune into it.

Joy is possible even in the hardest of times. If you confuse joy with finding happiness or satisfaction, you may be inclined to postpone its presence until you _____ , [fill in the blank with whatever you are working towards]. If you wait, you will find that: a) you squandered your possibility of joy now; and b) when you finally do achieve that dream, a new dream will have already replaced it and satisfaction, gratitude, and joy will continue to elude you. The consensus of the elderly is: Life is short and then you die.

Partnership of two autonomous beings who honor each other, are grateful to life, and have agreements for how to live helps us to en-joy our fleeting time on this plane.

Whom to Partner With

A shared dream isn't enough. To build a joyful life with someone, a potential partner must possess at least seven critical qualities. Among the hundreds of people I've surveyed, both single and coupled, the top seven MUST-HAVES for a partner come down to:

1. Autonomy – can stand on his/her own and is at peace in their sense of self

2. Hunger for learning – curious and secure enough to see gaining competence as a gift rather than a source of shame

3. Caring – acts with love and kindness

4. Trustworthy – reliable and authentic

5. Physical – sexual or not, the ability for tenderness

6. Emotional competence – deals with anger, non-violently, and appreciates the ironies of life and the capacity to laugh at ourselves

7. Grateful to life

With these seven qualities, you can build any kind of life you're interested in. (You'll note that neither money nor physical beauty made the cut.)

In speaking with a close family friend who was frustrated at her partner's lack of financial contribution, I asked if "autonomy" was a quality she required. I said that it's not a commandment that someone be autonomous. If she could accept that he was a dreamer and incompetent at making his daily bread, she could be happy with him. He didn't have the skills to generate regular work or a career. She cried and said, "He's trying." Trying does not equate to competence. Nor does it equate to learning. He did not take seriously that career is a domain of learning and, therefore, had no coach. He missed the boat on the first two critical requirements. Once she got clear that she indeed needed to be with someone who could contribute financially, she ended the two-year relationship.

What are your requirements? The journal at the end of this chapter is an invitation to create your own list. No matter what your list includes, as soon as you assess that your critical qualities are present in another – grab your partner and get ready to dance!

How to Partner

There is a distinct difference between partners and all other relationships – family, friends, or acquaintances In partnership, two (or more) autonomous individuals *declare* a commitment to co-create the future as equals. That means – each partner values the contribution of the other on a par with their own and takes 100% responsibility for making it work. Partnership is not a 50/50 deal. (50/50 or 40/60 is about money, not responsibility for making the partnership work.) Partnership brings forth a new unity. It comes into being when you both *declare*, **"Your concerns are my concerns"** (YCAMC). Words matter. Saying them aloud matters. Your speaking creates a stand in the world in which you affirm your commitment to have your partner's back and to be dedicated to supporting their wellbeing. These words birth a new energetic being – 'We' is born out of you and me.

YCAMC means: "I will support you in addressing your concerns." It does not mean: "I will want what you want." Concerns are not always easily defined. They underlie the desire. A Jaguar convertible, for example, is a want – only one way to take care of a concern for mobility or transportation.

YCAMC works as a structure only if it's mutually declared and partners are aligned on values. The partnership will last only as long as partners are committed to those concerns and adhere to their values. People and their concerns do change along the way. One very common breakdown in partnership occurs when partners change their minds or come into conflict about having a family, or not. This is often the basis for termination. Or it could be the basis for finding a way that supports disparate priorities.

By declaring YCAMC, you set the stage for navigating dances of difference. YCAMC requires a broader look at the concerns underneath the wants and finding new ways to address them. YCAMC asks that you create a larger context. In the simplest example - When He wants to eat barbecue and She wants Chinese – Mongolian barbecue could satisfy both. Of course, most differences aren't this easy. If you take YCAMC to heart, the declaration provides a path through conflict without the need to convince, push, or pull to get your way. It can take some time to find mutually satisfying conclusions. It took seven years for Cristián and me to find a coffee table that we both were delighted with.

Few people have ever declared YCAMC aloud. Without it, difference can be a bitch, a constant source of stress, resentment, and resignation. I ask if this mutual declaration has been made when couples get stuck in disagreement. A woman called in to a radio show I was on, asking for help in sorting out whether to stay married to her engineer husband of 30 years, a man with substantially different perspectives and desires. She wanted to be out in the world, engaging with people. His preference was to read, study, or watch TV.

When I asked if they had ever declared YCAMC, she gave me a common response. "Well," she hesitated, "We've never said those exact words, but we try to live that way." Trying doesn't get you there, especially when strong personal preference comes into play. Can you authentically say those words to another?

I gave her three additional questions to enable her to see the way to the future:

1. Do you care for each other enough to support the achievement of the life you each want?

2. Have you considered that partnership is a domain of learning?

3. Are you open to explore the possibility of improving the quality of your relationship?

If the answer to all three is YES, you have something to work with. It will take more than good intentions though. Committing to learn will require coaching, time, and practice.

Declaring your intention to understand and honor the concerns of the other is a good start to building a life with another human being in which you feel seen, appreciated, and cared for. Generous listening, without inserting your own agenda, is the way.

Daily Life

The reality of partnership is that daily life demands coordination, rules and boundaries and is built on a foundation of trust. If you want to build a safe, comfortable space to rest with another being, agreements about time, money, sex, and individual responsibilities create a sense of balance and being cared for. Alignment in equality, sex, time, money, and cohabitation is based on shared agreements. Promising is primary. We grow trust when we consistently do what we say we will. And even when we can't, we can continue to build trust by being in communication and managing our non-fulfillment.

Preparatory conversations are critical in bringing lives together. If they don't happen before you move in, they wind up being the source of acrimony when the relationship ends. Too many of my clients complain that they'd gotten the short end of the stick when they hadn't been clear. They have a tendency to try to negotiate after the fact.

Sharing a life presents practical concerns for balance and planning around family, friends, and allocations of time and space. Trust is built by telling the truth, keeping your promises, and managing them by communicating when you can't and making acceptable alternate arrangements.

What percentage of your time is devoted to individual concerns and how much for the partnership? One of the balancing challenges of cohabitation is determining where to live. One of my clients works in two cities in Pennsylvania several hours apart. What's important to them is that they have 4-5 nights per week together, so they are buying an apartment in the remote city and traveling together. In my world, our basic pattern is to go our separate ways most mornings and get together for dinner in the early evening. We generally plan more together time on the weekends.

Who will do what to take care of our space? What are our standards of neatness and comfort? Do we hire help? In our house dance, Cristián and I have developed a good balance. We make the bed together most mornings. I shop, cook, and launder. He cleans when I cook, as do I when he cooks. He vacuums, does the finances, cuts the grass, and fixes things. Sometimes we exchange roles and do them all, without resentment.

Entering a partnership, you automatically expand your close-in network. It becomes challenging to maintain a sense of balance with the pull and push of each other's well-established connections. My partnership with Cristián brought concerns for my mother, two daughters, and two brothers, and an ex-husband with HIV. Cristián was strongly linked to his daughter, mother, father, four siblings, and ex-wife. Our family network has continued to grow with grand-children, in-laws, ex-in-laws, nieces and nephews. To that delicate balance, we add our work and close friend connections. Dividing our time and attention often demands we make difficult choices. Where will we spend the holidays? How long can we each stay in foreign countries with family without threat of abandonment?

Bringing children into the mix presents a whole new set of questions for consideration – the values of parenthood. What are the actions of a good parent? What is the best way to teach your children? What are the rules? How do you deal with the children's failures? What are the roles in parenting step-children?

And perhaps more importantly, how do you care for the couple while you are raising kids? How will you keep the partnership juicy? Questions for alignment in the dance of parenting could fill another book. Asking these questions is beneficial because they help us define our desires, limitations, and potential disagreements. You can rest assured that your answers will be as individual as your own childhoods and are likely to spark strong emotion. Finding a path to agreement requires talking in constructive and responsible ways. For now, just hold onto the idea that the closer you are aligned in your perspectives, the more graceful your dance.

Sex

We long for physical connection. What kind works for you? Monogamy, non-monogamy, polyamory, or no sex?

While monogamy is still the norm, polyamorous relationships are on the rise. Accurate numbers are hard to come by, but Loving More – a polyamory support and advocacy organization – and Gallup polls note a steadily increasing polyamorous population. These relationships are not the same as other non-monogamous types, such as "swingers" or "don't ask/don't tell." Polyamory opens the space for consensual, ethical, and responsible intimate relationship with more than one partner, with the knowledge of all. This kind of relationship requires a strong commitment to honesty, integrity, equality, communication, and the willingness to have some awkward or difficult conversations. (The focus of Key Five – Dancing Naked – provides a structure for being honest and caring and producing positive outcomes when addressing emotionally charged issues.)

All sex is good sex as long as it's healthy sex, free of coercion, discrimination, and violence, and when all parties are happy with the arrangement.

Beyond orgasm, good sex includes the possibility of saying "no" without fear that the other will feel "rejected." It's inevitable that one partner will have a greater appetite than the other. "No" should be understood as: "Not now and remember that I love you and am open to you in the future."

If the sex isn't great, it's possible to make it so, if you remember that sex is a domain of learning and find coaches to support you. But even great sex is insufficient to hold a relationship together if there are no other points of shared interest and commitment. And great sex tends to disappear when other concerns surrounding money and family are not being adequately cared for, or playfulness is forgotten.

Money

Autonomous adults must be able to do the money dance – competently address the concerns for housing, food, transportation, and basic medical care. If the money dance isn't going well, the sex dance probably isn't either. The money dance is primary. It works well when the contributions of each partner is adequate for covering the basics. When you don't have to worry and plan around money, you can focus on other things.

To do the money dance well, you must be aligned about how you bring it in and how you spend it. Do you blend your money or maintain separate accounts? Without agreements, one partner is likely to feel resentful.

Merging money calls for agreements on individual contributions, a high level of trust for each other's approach to spending, and at least one person with enough financial competence to manage it. Either get someone who's competent to take care of your money for you, or learn how to care for it yourself. Because there is almost always a disparity on income production, money doesn't need to be a 50/50 deal. Even 30/70 can be the basis for balance if all parties assess fairness of other contributions. I may earn less, but I take responsibility for home schooling, for example. A feeling of imbalance needs to be recognized as a signal for help.

Making it Work

Your attitude about life may be your most vibrant quality – more important than the past, education, money, successes, failures, or circumstances. Life is 10% what happens to you and 90% your attitude about it. Every situation can be seen as either a burden or an opportunity. Whichever way you see it creates your attitude.

A good attitude reflects appreciation for the gifts you are given as well as a willingness to take on life's challenges.

Positive attitudes radiate confidence that life is working out. Can-do attitudes are contagious and self-perpetuating. A bad attitude pops up when you can't find the good and project your fear that things won't work out. The good news is – you can change your attitude. You actually have a choice about your attitude in every moment of the day. Even though attitudes are automatic, they can also be created. If things aren't working well and you're annoyed or frustrated, you could use an attitude adjustment. But before you can create it, you have to recognize it. If you have the wherewithal, take a pause and question your attitude. But honestly, it's sometimes hard to see yourself. In those moments, it's a tremendous gift to have a caring outside observer to let you know the attitude you are wearing.

The partnership is supported by an agreement to call out unproductive moods as long as you can do it in a way that is tender and non-threatening. "It looks like something is troubling you" could produce an opening for exploration. This delicate move is entirely dependent upon your capacity to listen and validate the concerns of the other.

If you notice worry, you might say, "How do you see the problem?" to make explicit the other's reality. Ask, "Are you open to seeing things differently?" Partnership provides the opportunity to see possibilities that the other has been blind to. But seeing differently is only possible if you're not attached to your view and committed to being right about it.

Traffic gives Cristián a very bad attitude, especially when he's driving, and sometimes he's not at all interested in changing his attitude. He just needs to be pissed off about the world screwing up his plans. Somehow it makes him feel more in control in a powerless situation. A different attitude could be possible if he were open to seeing the workings of "The Universal Timing Adjustor," the way that everything always works out in the end. He might be able to accept the gift of not going anywhere and listening to music or news, as if there were something important for him to hear at that moment. The only way to get there is by accepting the sucky mood and being open to change.

Traffic, breakdowns, and failures can quickly send your mood to hell in a handbasket. Developing competence in the emotional realm may be the most critical ability in restoring balance to the dance. We will work more deeply with moods and emotions as you progress through the book. In later chapters, I introduce practices for shifting attitudes and transforming difficult situations into opportunities for invention.

Journal:

This journal helps to shape your vision of a loving partner with whom to build a satisfying life and focuses on critical conversations for agreements.

1. List your critical qualities of a partner.

    a. Which seven are non-negotiable?

    b. Are there any of my seven qualities that you are willing to give up?

2. Are you autonomous?

    a. In what areas do you need help?

    b. Who can help you?

3. Loving what you do and being rewarded for sharing your gifts is a worthy life vision.

    a. Do you love your work?

    b. If not, are you committed to changing it?

    c. Who will support you in this concern?

4. If you're in a partnership, do you feel absolutely safe?

    a. If not, who have you told?

5. If you're in a partnership, have you declared Your Concerns Are My Concerns?

    a. If not, what's stopping you?

6. If you're in a partnership, how satisfied are you, on a scale of 1-10, with the sharing of responsibilities?

    a. If less than 10, what's missing?

    b. Can you make a request?

7. In other non-partner relationships, how satisfied are you, on a scale of 1-10, with the sharing of responsibilities?

    a. If less than 10, what's missing?

    b. Can you make a request?

8. Can you trust your partner to do what s/he says?

9. On a scale of 1-10, how satisfied are you with the sexual aspect of your relationship?

    a. If less than 10, what's missing?

    b. If sex is a critical quality for you, what request can you make to address this concern?

    c. Inasmuch as sex is a domain of learning, would you be open to coaching?

10. Are you comfortable with the amount of time you and your partner are apart?

    a. If not, why not?

    b. What requests can you make?

    c. Can you invite your partner to an exploration for a solution that would address your concerns?

KEY FIVE

Dance Naked

"If you look for truth you may find comfort in the end; if you look for comfort you will not get either comfort or truth, only soft soap and wishful thinking to begin, and in the end, despair."

–C. S. Lewis

YOU THINK YOU want intimacy? Ask yourself this question: "Do I want to be known and loved for who I truly am, in all my humanity, or do I want to be loved as the person I pretend to be?" Putting it that way makes it a no-brainer.

Intimacy – mutual openness to being known – is much more than sex because we are so much more than our sexuality. We dance in intimacy to experience the ecstasy of union – to lose the boundaries of our individuality and merge with the other. It's in this space that the "we" is created – that unique energetic being, born of conjoined individuals.

Intimacy is a constantly unfolding dance of self-discovery,

requiring profound authenticity, some courage or wildness of heart to go where you've never gone before, and trust – in yourself and your partners – that you are honored. The depth of your union is entirely dependent upon having a close personal relationship with the truth. Telling the truth – aligning what I think with what I say – has been a major learning focus in my life. I was born into lying.

My mother was a big liar. My younger brother was the issue of an affair she had when I was six months old. And that's just a small example. She was never sure if I was the child of her husband or his brother. I learned from her that withholding the truth – as long as you get away with it – is an effective, and fairly acceptable, practice for dealing with feelings of shame or fear, or of hurting the other (as long as you haven't killed somebody).

There's a tremendous cultural bias for withholding. Didn't your mother tell you, "If you don't have something good to say…" Just recently, my friend Kay shared with me that she had given some advice to a married friend of hers who'd had a minor indiscretion. He confessed to inexplicably kissing a woman (not his wife) on the beach. Kay said he was both horrified and remorseful. She felt proud of her sage guidance – the truth would only hurt his wife and he should suffer in silence. This is just classic! He used the excuse that his wife would be hurt to conceal his failure and avoid conflict.

In my twenties, I lied a lot. I told white lies to avoid confrontation and red lies about a couple of affairs in my first marriage. My lying continued after my first marriage fell apart. Even as I concluded that lying didn't work, I couldn't stop. My efforts towards truth-telling during my second marriage produced meager improvement. While my husband agreed to honesty in principle (although he insisted that omitting information was not lying), we both were incapable of handling the emotional fallout of any disappointing information. And there could be a lot of it, especially because for some time we chose to live in an open marriage with insufficient guidelines and agreements. I still lied to avoid uncomfortable conversations.

My excuse for this was that when I would try to raise intimate questions, he would refuse to talk about things and threaten to end the relationship. Feeling it was too risky to argue, I went away quietly. I'd lacked the courage to risk the relationship in pursuit of the truth. Had we known how to authentically talk about our fears, we might have arrived at the real truth – our life had become mundane together; sex with others produced a sense of aliveness that was absent, and we didn't have a clue about how to address it.

I needed to learn how to live truthfully.

What is True?

To tell the truth, you first have to know what the truth is. The philosophy of language taught me the difference between *THE* truth *with a capital T* (assertions) and *MY truth* (assessments). It was powerful to discover that THE truth is never good nor bad. It just is. I learned that a flat tire is just a flat tire. THE truth is the tire is flat. It's how you feel about it that brings forth its positive or negative quality.

If that strikes you as odd, consider this flat tire story: On October 17, 1989, I had a flat tire that prevented me from getting to a hair appointment. To be on time, I needed to be crossing the San Francisco Bay Bridge just in the moments that the 1989 World Series Earthquake struck and collapsed part of the upper level of the bridge. Good flat tire?

Learning that a tire can be both good and bad, I could see how multiple valid assessments (my truths) are possible about how things are in every situation. I became less attached to my own opinions and more eager to find useful interpretations.

But there was much deeper learning that I needed to do. I had no idea about how to break my habit of lying for convenience and avoidance. I found the help I needed on the very first pilgrimage of my 12-year Huichol path apprenticeship to a sacred mountain in northern California called Tatei Otlité. (In Huichol, Tatei means *grandfather or grandmother* god.)

On the map, Grandfather Otlité is Mt. Tamalpais, the great living being that forms the Golden Gate and the San Francisco Bay. Mt. Tam is an enormous living world unto itself, holding several microclimates. Its beaches, trails, meadows, and giant redwoods have been embraced and honored for millennia. For over 5,000 years, the Oloni and Mewok Indians regularly visited a secret sacred cave there to make offerings and ask for Otlite's renowned gifts of wisdom, protection, healing, weather, abundance, and relationship. Indigenous elders believe that his largesse supports us in moving in the world in a graceful and beneficial way. I was told that I could not receive Otlite's gifts with an insincere heart. Otlité demanded that we pilgrims give up lying altogether and live a completely honest life. I was being held accountable by a mountain. I would have to keep a record of every lie. If I didn't learn to live without lying, I could not progress on my path.

Ignorant of my ignorance, I didn't know how hard it would be until I began to keep a record of every lie that I committed. Lies like, "I didn't know I was speeding, Officer," or telling my mother that I'd be out of town so I could avoid having to see her were exceedingly challenging. As I recorded my deceptions, I had to ask myself, "What is your problem?" I saw that I wasn't willing to own my failures, that I dishonored the other by taking away their rightful reaction to a situation, and that I was incapable of addressing the hurt feelings that resulted from my actions.

I began to see that every time I lied or withheld my feelings, I inflicted a wound to the relationship. Some little piece of myself became barricaded. I saw that in my past relationships, wounds accrued, bonds weakened, and we found very good reasons for acquiring other dance partners – all to conceal my shame and fear. Discomfort is what makes the hard truth hard. Otlité backed me into a corner and forced me to look at the parts of myself that I wanted to disown – my incompetence and disregard for others.

Radical Authenticity

"In wise love, each divines the high secret self of the other…"

–W. B. Yeats

With practice (it took a few years), I achieved a level of honesty I call "radical authenticity." To live radically authentic with another human being is not an issue of morality nor a commandment. It's a requirement for me to let myself go, with nothing to hide – to dance naked – with others who want to dance naked with me. It's not necessarily for everyone.

The best way to learn to dance naked is in partnership, with someone who's committed to master the dance of intimacy. Cristián was the perfect partner. He preferred to stand on the solid ground of truth rather than on a stage of spun sugar, even in the face of disappointment. We created 'radical authenticity' in our relationship by **declaring** to each other, "I will tell you everything I don't want to tell you." And then the fun began.

Living as his word, after one year of marriage, Cristián presented me with a radically authentic bombshell – that he no longer wanted to be monogamous. Apparently, our falling in love period was officially over.

I should have expected something like this from a man who was 14 years my junior, who had missed the era of sex, drugs, and rock and roll, married as a virgin at 24, and had experienced very few sexual encounters before we'd met. I could appreciate his desire. I was long over the abundance of casual sex in the 70's. My history told me that hot sex lasted only so long before it cooled and became empty.

There was nothing I could say to convince him it was a bad idea. His fantasies had taken over the controls. I knew that he couldn't exorcise them just because he wanted to. This wasn't a philosophical conversation. He had to learn for himself the hard way – through experience.

I assessed I would lose him if I insisted on monogamy. My choice was either to live with a man who wanted to have sex with others or live without him. Both scenarios made me fearful. Clearly this was not the dream of marriage I had hoped for, but it was the reality I got. Above all, I was grateful for the truth. It enabled me to make my own decisions about how I wanted to live, and it served to deepen our intimacy.

I could tolerate his desire for sex, but I drew the line at looking for love. I was willing to continue the relationship and take on his concern for exploration if I could trust that he was being honest about not wanting another love relationship. On that basis, we worked to establish agreements that would allow us to both feel safe.

The first few were easy: Honesty/full disclosure – I wanted to know about it and trust that he would straightforwardly answer whatever questions I had. I also asked for a commitment to safe sex and no entanglement with friends or co-workers.

We stumbled in making one final agreement – I asked for the same freedom for myself. Although I was not particularly interested in outside sex, I needed him to experience the same courage, vulnerability, and lack of possessiveness that was required in an open marriage. "No way, I am a Latin man" was his initial reaction. But his commitment to take my concerns as his own (YCAMC) forced him to confront his macho thinking. It took some time before we reached agreement. But in some moment, he recognized his hypocrisy and saw that he had to let go of his possessiveness – just as I had. As we worked earnestly to stretch our capacity to trust, our relationship was growing right through the middle of the challenge.

When he shared about his first liaison, I was truly relieved. His revelation also included, "Honestly, I don't know what I was making such a big deal about."

While his exploration continued beyond this one experience, through it he came to assess these extracurricular activities as distracting and shallow; that a sacred union is a profound journey of the human spirit. Having spoken his truth without shame and accepting the consequences of his actions, he created the opportunity for monogamy to return to our relationship – not because Mother Culture said we should, but for the sake of an exploration of intimacy.

I don't want to suggest that this situation was easy for me. I had never lived with this level of honesty before. Some of my friends called me courageous. Others called me stupid. The majority said they could never do what I was doing. But living day by day, staying in the present rather than projecting a future of loss, listening with my heart, and moving slowly through the experience made it possible for me to live with a terribly uncomfortable truth. The level of trust we were building makes a cover-up like, "I bought it on sale" ridiculous.

How willing are you to live with this level of honesty? If not, why not?

The Critical Truth

"Politeness is the poison of partnership."

–Edwin Land

Relationship, of any kind, makes you well-positioned to reflect the greatness as well as the weakness of others. While sexual candor may look challenging, showing a friend or partner his or her frailty for a partner may be even more so. Enduring relationship demands that you talk about what's not working in your dance together. You must make critical assessments. What I mean by "critical" is important or vital rather than unfavorable, derogatory, or bad.

Radical authenticity is the commitment to talk about how you see things, especially the difficult stuff, for the sake of the partnership – the stuff you've probably lied about or omitted in the past to avoid the discomfort. These conversations have historically been hard because many people react badly to a different opinion, they may feel completely invalidated, or they have delicate egos, easily bruised when they discover that they're not doing as well as they hoped.

Competence in the dance of intimacy is demonstrated by your ability to have these critical conversations in a way that inspires cooperation rather than defensiveness. This is entirely possible if you can get rid of your own negative energy first. Understanding the nature of assessments – that they are not THE truth and only one of a number of possible interpretations – makes it possible to unhook from the negativity, speak more authentically, and listen with openness.

Remember – the truth of any situation is a combination of assertions and assessments which are neither positive nor negative. To the extent that you believe that the situation shouldn't be the way it is, you bring negativity. To the extent that your assessment is made for the sake of strengthening the 'we' – without blame or make-wrong – you create a clean space for an honest conversation.

Remembering that there are multiple ways of looking at anything minimizes defensiveness. Being unattached to your reality removes the energy of righteousness. If you don't have to be right about something, you won't position the other to be wrong. Being able to say, "This is just my opinion and I'd like to hear how you see things," eases the way.

But before you can deliver critical assessments, it's

important to develop your own capacity to receive them. Your ability to tell others what you really think in a caring and respectful way directly correlates to your own competence to accept criticism. I find that people tend to vastly overrate their capacity, saying that they appreciate "constructive" criticism. But that usually amounts to being able to accept rather impersonal or technical training on how to do something better in the work domain. Domains of competence such as *parenting, communication, body/health/food, listening, and emotions* are often hot buttons for critical assessment and potential defensiveness triggers.

Seeking Critical Assessments

I asked a successful business manager whom I was coaching, "If you asked your wife, 'on a scale of 1-10, 10 being perfectly satisfied, how satisfied are you with our relationship,' what would she say?" He responded, "Oh man, I'd be afraid to ask."

Why not? What is there to dread? What are you afraid to lose? It usually comes down to "identity." We just hate to look bad or lose face. Consider again the "looking-good syndrome" (Key One).

The inability to make critical assessments to a partner is one of the biggest barriers to intimacy. It may be an indication that the partner is not a dedicated learner. Critical assessments are always easier for learners. Learners aren't so fragile because they are constantly seeking ways to improve. Anyone committed to excellence is compelled to find value in someone pointing out a way to improve their dance. Assessments that come from a desire to support another's learning are generally more well-received.

You can receive a critical assessment in a curious, open way when you are clear about the difference between an assertion and an assessment. It is easier to hear what the other has to say when you know that an assessment is just one of many possible interpretations. As long as you understand there is never just one correct assessment, hearing something that doesn't line up with the way you see the world, you can say, "That's curious. Tell me more."

What Are You Afraid Of?

Imagine the worst things someone could say to you. You're lazy, crazy, stupid, sloppy, uncaring, or some variation? If any of those words are said in anger, they are unlikely to open the door to change. But if you can look beneath the unkind labels, and if you're being honest, you can find some ways you've demonstrated all these qualities. Authentic self-examination will show that each of us possesses all human qualities – and their opposite. We all have some degree of ambition and laziness; authenticity and inauthenticity, impeccability and sloppiness, stinginess and generosity, gratitude and apathy; intelligence and stupidity, strength and weakness, and so on. In peaceful and centered moments, we can usually own them all and laugh unreservedly as we recount stories of our trials, naiveté, incompetence, and jerkiness. The fact is: We can always find some validity in what the other is saying – if we have nothing to defend.

Knowing this, how can you claim that you are not any particular way? The question is not IF you are, but rather, HOW MUCH you are being that way and if it is impeding your joy. And "how much" requires you develop some standards. How much room for lateness will you allow before you embrace the assessment "unreliable?" Is 10 minutes late twice in a month OK? Without standards, you are likely to get stuck in a perfection model with no appreciation for improvement.

"You're always on the phone" has got to be untrue; likewise, "You never pick up your socks." 'Always' and 'never' are assertions guaranteed to produce an oppositional response. "You're frequently late" is an assessment you can work with. Change is possible when you look for grounding. How often have you been late? What assertions can be made about past history? Is there any room for lateness? Why is this an issue? For the sake of what are you even having the conversation?

Be alert to 'should' conversations. Any statement that includes a 'should' is going to be problematic. The 'shoulds' are best received from people with expertise, to whom you've granted authority. Keep in mind that while there may be sufficient grounding for an expert's assessments, they still don't represent THE truth in The World. Even the best doctors make terrible assessments. We all do. Yet there's still a good reason for being open.

The best outcome in a critical assessment conversation is that all parties feel heard and understood. Your job as the listener is to put your righteousness aside, listen with your heart rather than your ego, be willing to see through another's eyes, and authentically say, "I can get why you say that." This doesn't mean, "You're right," or "I agree with you," or that anything needs to change. It simply means, "I understand where you're *coming from* and how the world looks to you."

After further consideration, you can choose to work with whichever assessment offers the greatest possibilities for improvement. As a culture, we tend to seek the positive assessments, the ones we like. "You're such a good writer" is a nice example. It doesn't point to the opportunity of learning. But a critical one, "I think you really would benefit from a writing course," opens possibilities for a different future.

With nothing to defend, you are free to determine if there is anything you want to change. Listening to another's truth, you have the opportunity to rectify wrongs, improve effectiveness, or clarify misunderstandings. To be shown an area of blindness is a gift if it is given in a context of caring.

Speaking the Critical Truth

A commitment to radical authenticity is not a license, or requirement, to broadcast every thought that you have. Critical assessments are advice, and advice is an offer. Any time you have an important and possibly difficult assessment, your first move is to make an offer like, "Are you interested in some feedback?" or "Would you like my opinion?" The critical truth is best spoken by someone who is more interested in transforming a situation than being right. Sharing your infinite wisdom without invitation is one of the biggest missteps in the dance of relationship.

My mother once complained to me that her aide had a bad attitude after they had gotten into a tussle over "the best route to get to her apartment." Because the aide was frequently late, my mother suggested that she take two buses instead of one for a faster journey. Mom couldn't understand why the aide was pissed off. I asked her if she had asked the aide if she would like to hear her opinion about it. My mother said, "Of course not. Why would I do that? What if she said 'no'?" "Then," I suggested, "you'd have to keep your mouth shut." My mother did not like that idea at all. She's not unique in this regard. So many of us are confident that we are so smart and right about things, we just blurt them out, willy-nilly.

If you position the conversation as your desire to contribute, and the listener has accepted your offer, your critical assessment is much more likely to be received with openness.

Your assessment could still sting. A difficult truth might be, "You're not bringing in enough money." You create a positive environment for change if you come to the conversation from the perspective of the 'we.' When you come from the belief (assessment) that the situation shouldn't be the way it is, you bring blame. You may frame this assessment by asking, "Are you open to looking at our financial situation with me?"

It's worth repeating: If you haven't dismantled your own negative feeling, don't try to peddle your assessment for the good of the other. And if you can't let go of your negative feelings, at least get honest about them. Radical authenticity is a call to acknowledge your feelings, childish as they may be. When the hard truth triggers a feeling of being wounded and defensiveness, intimacy recedes, and conflict is often sparked. Coming from the 'we' and without blaming the other for the situation, you are able to lead the listener in an intimate dance of exploration. You can dance naked.

Journal:

1. With whom would you like to learn to dance naked?

2. How do you assess your relationship to the truth? On a scale of 1-10, how honest are you?

3. Begin to take note of each of your lies and document what you were protecting.

4. Where do you tend to withhold your truth?

5. What are the honest assessments you would prefer to avoid hearing?

6. Ask one of your closest friends, "How do you see that I can be more effective in my life?"

7. Ask another friend or work colleague, "What do you think is important for me to change about the way I operate?"

8. Have you listened to someone telling you that they are dissatisfied with what you did without defending or justifying?

   a. How have you responded to a complaint or suggestion that something you're doing is unhealthy or annoying?

Karen Aberle

9. With whom have you had a recent disagreement?

    a. What was your assessment?

    b. What was the other's assessment?

    c. Why was it said?

    d. What evidence was provided to support the assessment?

    e. How did it resolve?

10. Instead of, "I disagree," begin to substitute, "Tell me more," or "Why do you say that?"

    a. What do you notice?

KEY SIX

Dance with Conflict

*"When we are carried away by our fear
and prejudices, we cannot listen to others.
We cannot just bring two sides together
around a table to discuss peace when
they are still filled with anger, hatred
and hurt. If you cannot recognize your
fear and anger, if you do not know how to
calm yourself, how can you sit at a peace
table with your enemy?"*

–Thich Nhat Hanh

IN THE CONTEXT of partnership, or close relationships in
general, difference is inevitable. You can expect alter-
native realities when discrete identities with unique
histories, interests, and perspectives come together. Even with
a strong foundation of shared values, life presents plenty of
opportunity to experience difference of opinions and priorities, significant and mundane.

Difference comes with the declaration, "I don't see it that

way." This is not necessarily a problem when you can agree to move in different directions in peace, honoring the other's perspective. Even political difference, so often a breaking point for couples, is workable (think Mary Matalin and James Carville). Fighting about different opinions becomes ridiculous when you appreciate the distinction of assertion v. assessment. We can never debate our assessments into THE truth.

Difference evolves into conflict when it includes anger – the powerful, uncomfortable, and hostile response to a perceived provocation, hurt, or threat. Hostility is the critical element. Conflict is born of the clash of self-protecting energies. It's one of the ways we discover who we are as separate individuals in the web of our interconnectedness. Conflict always creates 'the other.'

However challenging, conflict can be a doorway to deep relationship and a spark for transformation. It is an alert that some change is necessary. If you don't recognize conflict as a creative force, you will remain embattled and isolated. It's ironic because it looks like the conflict itself is keeping you apart but, really, it's your unwillingness to engage in it. In conflict aversion, you will unwittingly construct a dry, predictable relationship with plenty of storage space for withheld communications. The key is to learn to work with anger.

About Anger

To be human is to have anger. Even the holiest among us have it. Anger can arise when our boundaries have been breached; we feel ourselves attacked, disregarded, disdained, or taken advantage of; when we feel damaged by others who don't keep their word, or act above the law.

Anger comes before thought. It's primal. Anger erupts from the depths of your being, like lava, ready to decimate everything in its path. It wants to be expressed – to lash out, to punish, and seek retribution.

Many people have difficulty dealing with anger. Depending upon the depth of the perceived hurt, anger comes in mild and extra-hot varieties. Mild anger might sound indignant, "How dare you?" Heated fury can sound like, "You bitch, you've ruined my life," or even, "I hate you." Your family of origin has shaped your automatic response to these expressions. If your tendency is to withhold or conceal it for the sake of peace, you will pay a great price.

Stuffing it never really works because the hurt won't go away by itself. Anger festers. Suppression may ultimately result in a nuclear-grade explosion. Or, if you've succeeded at keeping it in, bottled-up anger can result in depression or disease. Unresolved, every unanswered hurt becomes a wound. Before long, scars form. Numbness and a need for self-protection begin to dismantle the foundation of the partnership. If a relationship is to endure with joy and passion, you must address your hurts and anger. However the anger is expressed, it is a call to reconcile realities, repair damage, restore balance, and strengthen connection. Anger is always accompanied by opportunity. It is an invitation to a dance of transformation of the 'we.'

Sitting in the fire of strong emotion with another human being for the sake of deepening the relationship is a learnable skill. In indigenous communities, conflict is recognized as a gift of spirit that forces us to stretch further than we ever thought imaginable; a call to abandon the need for control and discover that if we are connected to our hearts, flying is possible. You have to jump into the void and bring your fear with you rather than waiting for it to dissipate. People who embody this wisdom are sacred warriors. Their capacity to unite us through the challenges and messiness of living together makes life more wondrous and satisfying for anyone they touch.

The dance of conflict is a dance you can master. Like the tango, it takes two – but you only need one person to lead.

The Moves of the Dance of Conflict

"An eye for an eye will only make the whole world blind."

–M. K. Gandhi

Dancing with conflict takes a different approach to anger management. The first move is to name it. Conflict often sweeps us up into its uncomfortable dance before we've even heard the invitation or know what's going on. It might sound silly to say, "I see we have a conflict here," but this declaration, however it is said, can produce a momentary separation from the action and remind the combatants of the rules of engagement – the commitments you've already made in peace time. Your commitment to *radical authenticity* demands the anger be brought to the floor, however ugly it may be. The only way to enter the dance is to speak your truth. Your commitment to *Honoring your Partner* is to hold space for difference. Your commitment to hold *Your Concerns Are My Concerns* recalls the 'we.' This translates into: Your anger is our concern, even if it's directed at me. Two additional declarations are: *I accept conflict as a natural human dimension* and *I am committed to non-violence.*

The dance is likely to begin with an angry outburst – a declaration that conveys the hurt, damage, or offense. This invitation can sound more or less threatening. A masterful dance partner can initiate a dance of conflict by tuning in to a brewing, unspoken complaint, perhaps in the tone of the other's voice or facial expression. When you sense anger on the horizon, it's best to encourage its expression. Developing the capacity to observe its unfolding and naming it "conflict" before the lashing out is a key to disarmament. The sooner, the better, the less explosive. Your ability to receive the outburst/invitation depends on where you come from – your history with strong emotion. Some families and cultures are more comfortable stepping into conflict than others.

However it starts, when the pain is exposed, the dance is on. Traditionally, the angry partner has set the pace, but the dance can be much more effectively led by the listener. Whoever is the first to **declare**, "We can resolve this," takes the lead in the dance. Knowing these moves, you open the flow of transformative energy and produce change.

De-escalation

Anger is a nasty hook. Feeling attacked, you are likely to be propelled into defensive mode. A competent leader knows that anger cannot be overcome by more anger, only by compassion, recognizing the pain underneath the wrath. Eric Hoffer, an American social writer, author of *The Ordeal of Change*, says that anger is the prelude to courage. Anger, yes. Rage, no. Competence in leading requires the capacity to unhook and center – to be at choice about your response rather than pushed or pulled by emotion.

At center, there is a palpable stillness that allows for observation, reflection, and choice. Centering is a mindful practice in which you intentionally focus on your breathing while moving your energy away from the top of your head (or your fists) to a spot two inches below your navel. Regular meditation helps build muscle memory for centering. When you are centered, you can move left, right, up, or down. Center is the place of optimum possibilities. With your feet on the ground, honor your partner, acknowledge the anger, and **request** a pause to create a listening space.

Early on, Cristián and I were caught in a disastrous pattern. If I got angry with him, he would deflect and invalidate my position, and I would get angrier, to the point where he would get calmer and calmer (not to be confused with more and more centered) and say, "Look at yourself; you're a hysterical, raging maniac." Then, he would disengage for some period of time, often a couple of days. These encounters produced wounds that became easier and easier to reopen.

Rather than, "Get a hold of yourself," which has an escalating quality, the leader must create space for the anger, sit with the discomfort, allow for it to be spoken in a forceful way, with a boundary established for demeaning language, another escalator. The leader looks to validate the anger rather than make the expression of it wrong. You have to listen to the story that has created the madness. "I want to hear how it is for you" is a **request** that immediately begins to deescalate the conflict. You can do this when you return to your commitment to YCAMC. You have to hear the concerns so that you can determine how best to provide support.

Creating the Listening Space

The tale is still told that many years ago in the Catskill Mountains, a dispute arose between the Mohawk and Oneida peoples. When the two groups couldn't agree to sit down and talk together, an Onondaga shaman was called in to help. The shaman tuned in to the energies of the land and found a place of balance, a spot on a stream in which a perfect ice circle formed. It is said that the land itself blessed them with the openness that made peace possible. Tales aside, we all know some places are more supportive for conversation than others – maybe the couch instead of the kitchen, a park bench instead of a restaurant. The leader should move the dance there.

The leader **declares,** "I come here to work towards resolution. I will listen to what you have to say. I will speak my truth and am open to recognize that it may not be THE truth. I will not threaten you or resort to violence if I don't get my way. I know this may not be a short process and will work until we arrive at some improvement, even if that takes days, weeks, or years." Commitments to *Honor, YCAMC,* and *Radical Authenticity* in the background make this a real possibility. Then, let the listening begin, being mindful of the difference between assertions and assessments.

Listening – Let All Sides Be Heard

Knowing that another may honestly see things differently, each person in turn needs to state fully and unflinchingly their position, without interruption. Some native people sit in a circle, passing a talking stick, a ritual object that symbolizes the equality of everyone and entitles the speaker as much time as needed to speak their peace. The talking stick works for just two people as well. The generous listening practice in Key Three develops your capacity to give your undivided attention. Get the whole story out. Don't try to set the record straight point by point, moment by moment.

It is powerful when the leader of the dance can distinguish assertions from assessments and separate out 'what happened' from 'how it felt' and 'why it happened.' What happened, for example, was, "You didn't answer me." "You ignored me" is an interpretation. How it felt is a result of the story made up by the offended party about why.

The process of speaking and listening alone often resolves many conflicts. Once all sides have spoken, there may be an opportunity to clarify mistakes, misunderstandings, or misinformation. We can release anger more quickly when we accept that damage was produced by accident rather than intention. When something gets broken, knowing that it was inadvertent rather than deliberate can make a huge difference. Repetitive "accidents" indicate a deeper issue. They cannot be constantly excused and are a call for reexamination.

Speaking – I Can See Why You Say That

If you are being accused, can you find an ounce of validity in what your accuser is stating? So much of our conflict is centered on self-defense. What happens when we don't have to defend or justify or take the offensive?

Here's a common conflict: "I'm angry because you don't spend enough time with me." Here are three common responses:

Defense: "Yes, I do."

Justification: "What do you want me to do, quit my job?"

Counter-attack: "You're never satisfied."

If you listen with your heart without the need for protection, with a commitment to looking out through another's eyes, you can usually understand why they are saying what they're saying. Understanding where they are coming from does not concede that their perspective is right. It does, however, allow you to feel their pain.

The key move in the dance of conflict is being able to authentically **declare**, "I can see why you say that." "You've been alone quite a bit lately," validates the other's perspective and de-escalates. It takes you to the ground floor of the issue and opens a door to someplace new.

Few of us have developed the capacity to regularly de-escalate. And when we can't, we stay woefully stuck in the conflict, trying to convince the other that they're wrong. Cristián and I were stuck in a classic, constant, ridiculous, and potentially dangerous conflict for years. It all had to do with driving, a common issue for couples.

Men and women, or partners in general, often have different driving styles. The driver usually feels more comfortable than the passenger, connected to the road, with a handle on the controls. The passenger seat can be particularly unnerving for anyone with a need for control or a different approach to the road.

As a frequent passenger, I tried to mask my fear. If I asked him to slow down or create more distance from the car in front, he listened to it as an insult – an uninvited criticism of his driving competence – producing a flash conflict.

Addressing my concerns would constitute a loss of an important battle. While he got very quiet, his actions screamed loudly, "If you don't be quiet, I will show you what a good driver I am by zigging and zagging through traffic at high speed," which only served to escalate. Feeling resentful at being treated with such disrespect, and from a powerless position, I would begin to cry. More escalation. Fury, radiating from both of us, my last-ditch effort – demand he stop and let me out, which, of course, he wouldn't. And so, the conflict between us would spin out of control until the coup de grâce – he refused to engage in any conversation.

This scenario was a regular part of our lives before Cristián and I had committed to care for the other's concerns. It was perhaps the most challenging conflict we'd had. (That might sound like an exaggeration considering the other difficult situations we faced, but this driving thing touched such deep fears in both of us.)

De-escalation began as soon as I shifted my interpretation of his refusal to engage with me from 'punishment' to 'silence is a good idea' – as long as his refusal to talk was temporary. In the heat of conflict, calling for a break is a potent and cooling tactic. It provides an opportunity for emotions to return to a workable level. The question is: How much time do you need to calm down? Normally, after a pause, one of us will come to the resolution table with a genuine invitation, "Can we try this again?" indicating our willingness to listen more. With practice, the time we needed for cooling became shorter and shorter.

When I generously listened, I could see why he felt that

I was challenging his competence as a driver. At that point, I could honestly acknowledge that I trusted his abilities. In all of our years together, he has never been part of a collision with another car. Taking up my side, he could understand my body's automatic fear reaction triggered by fast moves cutting through traffic or the unexpected blast of a horn from a nearby car marking its territory. While my mind could trust his skill, my body couldn't.

Picking up the other's side, seeing why they say what they say, begins to melt our icy, protective shields. From the place of feeling our shared pains, we can explore how to design a way to take care of both of us. While we know that the automatic triggering will undoubtedly continue, we are practicing to use it as a reminder for what we are committed to. With time, we've been able to restore balance more quickly.

Yet even experienced warriors may not always be able to work through stubborn conflicts on their own. How long do you have to struggle before you ask for help from someone with competence?

When You Can't Hear

Persistent and recurrent conflicts call for outside help. Sitting in the fire of conflict takes practice and support. When you just can't get out of your own perspective to see the validity of another's, it is beneficial to have people you can call on to help you see what you are blind to and monitor your improvement.

Indigenous elders are responsible for maintaining the balance of the community. Disputes are brought before them and are resolved in short order. Westerners have psychologists, coaches, therapists, and friends who are competent to expand our vision. But with a strong foundation of Western individualism, people are prone to keep their conflicts private and attempt to gut it out alone.

Early in our relationship, Cristián and I got terribly stuck in a conflict, an irreconcilable difference that left us stuck in disdain, disgust, dishonor, and resentment. We couldn't see our way out and resigned ourselves to this base level diminishment, living for years with a constant annoyance, agreeing to disagree. But in truth, this way of dealing (or really, not dealing) maintained a wound in our relationship.

We had very different standards of neatness around the house. Trained as an engineer (and by an exceptionally fastidious and organized mother), Cristián expected impeccability in our living space. He assessed me as sloppy, would get angry, and linger in a bad mood if he came home to find cups in the sink or piles on my desk.

I viewed him as obsessive/compulsive. He vacuumed every day, sometimes twice a day. The noise of the vacuum grated on my nerves. He defended, "I don't believe in brooms and I'm proud of it." Really. He said that. I did what other righteous people do – amassed support for my position. My friends agreed (even if they were a tiny bit jealous) that he was unreasonably picky.

Tired of the constant battle, we enlisted the help of a coach who focused us on our objections about the other. Our coach proposed that what was keeping us stuck was our own disowned and disdained qualities. I would never want to see myself as obsessive/compulsive and he abhorred sloppiness.

She asked me if there was any domain in my life that I was obsessive about. My answer was immediate – communication. I can't stand to have messy communication and am compulsive about cleaning it up. And where was Cristián lax or sloppy? Communication. He often had a "deal with it later" attitude, especially when conversations got uncomfortable.

It was revelational. As soon as both of us could accept the frailty or incompetence in ourselves, we had room for the needs and preferences of the other. The dark spot of our relationship was illuminated and the conflict began to disappear. I became less irritated by the sound of the vacuum, and he was more inclined to pick up a sponge without resentment. Compassion arises as we begin to see through the eyes of the other. When we're in a place of really listening, we can embark on a design for mutual satisfaction.

All this sounds very civilized and simple. And it is. But it's not easy. Humans are perturbable beings who get triggered instantaneously, lash out, and set off a seemingly endless cycle of anger and blame.

Having mutual commitments to *Honor, YCAMC, Radical Authenticity, Learning*, and *Nonviolence* make it possible to hang in through the pain and enable conflict as a source of transformation. Faith in the process is built with each experience of partners honoring their stands and keeping their word. Learning how to dance in conflict with people we know and love prepares us to go out in the world and manage the conflict with strangers.

It only takes one person to de-escalate conflict. The one who can create the listening space and has the willingness to see things from the other's perspective can lead the dance back into equilibrium. Compassion is a natural outcome. In the process of resolving conflict, you may find that you produced damage and need to apologize. The next chapter – Creating Passion (again) - explores the moves of apology and forgiveness to restore wholeness and reconnect to the frequency of joy.

Journal:

This journal is in support of learning to deal with anger and difference.

1. Whom have you fought with? About what?

2. What do you need to be right about?

3. Do you share a commitment to resolve all conflicts to a satisfactory conclusion?

4. Do you find yourself capable of asking for a break to let strong emotion subside?

5. Are you able to set aside your righteousness and listen generously?

6. Can you see why the other feels the way they do? Is there even 1% of their assessment that is valid?

7. If the conflict is unresolved, what commitments can you make and ask for to continue the dance?

8. Can you accept that sometimes people are incompetent, get triggered, and act badly without doubting their affection?

9. Do you require an apology? Do they? Is it forthcoming?

KEY SEVEN

Create Passion (Again)

"There is a candle in your heart, ready to be kindled. There is a void in your soul, ready to be filled. You feel it, don't you?"

–Rumi

Passion is a compelling enthusiasm for something or someone, a strong and barely controllable emotion that overtakes you. Passion is a hunger for returning to the dance.

In the early stages of love, passion happens, beyond your control. Everything seems to work seamlessly. But you won't dance that easily together forever. As the relationship matures, you will blunder. You will hurt. You will take yourself away. But if the relationship is to endure, passion can and must be created and recreated. To give rise to passion, you must make mutual satisfaction a priority, take responsibility for toe-mashing, and be a source of joy.

To love is to act with a concern for the peace and satisfaction of the other. When you can do that for another at the same time as you are satisfying yourself, you come together. You become together. The more you create satisfaction with your partners, the more trust you develop, the stronger your bonds, the more you seek return engagements. Who better to be with?

Taking the other for granted is a pervasive malady of long-term relationships. Mundane chores and external pressures deaden passion. You have the opportunity to reawaken it when you start paying attention to the abundant dances you are performing.

Inasmuch as every dance that you do in life has a beginning, middle, and end, every end is an opportunity to experience peace, satisfaction, and gratitude. There are dances within dances. The dance of "dinner," for example, begins with an offer to share a meal and ends when you move on to the next activity. But within that dance, there may be a number of component dances, such as shopping, ordering or cooking, and cleaning. Each dance provides another chance to be satisfied and express appreciation.

Taking the lead in a dance is to be responsible for ensuring that partners are clear about what satisfaction would look like when it's done. The goal is to close each dance in the embrace of your partner. Envision the joy of a satisfying dance when it's done. It might look like the dip Fred Astaire makes with Ginger Rogers. They glow with appreciation. In our busy world, we frequently close with a perfunctory, or even implied, "thanks." We then move on too quickly. You shortchange yourself and your partner if you don't pause for gratitude, take the time to express your appreciation in a way that is really heard. A full expression of gratitude includes an acknowledgement of what specifically was done and what it meant to you. When honestly expressed, it is unlikely that you will ever do it too much. Expressing gratitude – to life, to others for more than what they do but for who they are – makes you a most attractive dance partner, someone the world loves to dance with.

Returning to Gratitude

Gratitude can be hard to manifest when you are disappointed, mistakes were made, promises broken, or feelings were hurt. The absence of gratitude is resentment. As long as you are stuck in it, you will be isolated.

If you are living fully, it is guaranteed that you will fail. Apology and/or forgiveness are moves that release the negative emotions that keep you locked in a cell of past grievance. They open the door to learning and transformation and restore the 'we.'

When you fail and see the damage that was produced, and accept responsibility for your situation, you can apologize. With an apology, you validate the other's perspective. When offered authentically, apology is a powerful move to dismantle anger, de-escalate conflict, and begin to assuage the pain you caused. In choosing to be responsible for some damage, apology is a move to heal the wound. Once you have restored emotional balance, you can find ways to address the concerns that separated you in the first place and move towards closure, peace, and satisfaction.

Without pride, you can apologize for almost anything. Regardless of what happened, you can find your part in producing the damage, even if it is to think what you might have done differently. "I'm sorry that I didn't anticipate your difficulty" is one such apology.

How to Apologize

"It takes a great deal of character strength to apologize quickly out of one's heart rather than out of pity. A person must possess himself and have a deep sense of security in fundamental principles and values in order to genuinely apologize."

–Stephen Covey

"I'm sorry" comes more easily to learners. Without permission to be a learner, mistakes are hard to own up to, especially if you are insecure about your place in the world and are afraid that your rank will be further diminished by acknowledging clumsiness or stupidity.

Apology is also easier for those who see themselves as part of life's interconnectedness. They recognize a wound to the other as a persistent wound to themselves and the entire web. Without that awareness, an apology may not appear important.

You declare apology in a conciliatory tone. ("I'm sorry" said with an ounce of anger does not qualify as an apology.) "I'm sorry" is a good start, but as a standalone expression, it doesn't say quite enough. In a powerful apology, you acknowledge responsibility for your part in producing damage, express appreciation for the cost or emotional impact, and seek to restore trust by offering to compensate for any damage you may have caused and committing not to repeat the damaging act. Abusers often damage, apologize, and damage again. Without the commitment and capacity to not repeat, the apology is vacant and best not be accepted.

Is there someone to whom you owe an apology? You can't undo anything you have already done, but you can face up to it. Bow to your partner, tell the truth, and declare responsibility. Offer to make up for the loss to bring back the equilibrium in the dance. Use the lesson. Ask for acceptance of your apology and be prepared not to get it because, like any offer, the listener is free to decline.

Forgiveness

"To forgive is to set a prisoner free and discover the prisoner was you."

—Lewis B. Smedes

Acceptance of an apology is forgiveness. Seeing yourself in the other and having compassion for their failures, you can forgive. Forgiveness is the healing energy that closes the wound and allows for the return of flow in our dance together. It makes for a graceful conclusion. Forgiveness is a gift – a must for enduring relationships. When you share a commitment to each other's concerns, finding forgiveness is essential to your own health and well-being. When you do, you return to 'we.' To forgive is to declare, "I will no longer hold this against you. At the same time, I do not promise to forget."

Sometimes an apology isn't accepted for several possible reasons. Perhaps the expression didn't really line up with the perspective of the hurt party, or the offer of compensation was not assessed to be fair. Maybe the apology didn't include a commitment not to repeat. In those cases, you have some more dancing to do.

Some people don't want to accept an apology because they believe it gives them leverage. Some withhold forgiveness for the sake of punishment. These are the most difficult dances to close with gratitude. If your partner declines your apology and makes no commitment to revisit the conversation, you must accept that decision with honor. This is its own form of closure. Passion wanes when hurts go unresolved.

If your apology is declined, as the leader of the dance, you may ask, "What can I do to make things right with you?" A common answer is, "Time." Some people are slower to cool than others. They just need to be quiet and process out the anger. How much time is acceptable depends on your tolerance for dancing alone, for letting the conversation rest in a state of incompletion. Patience is possible with a commitment to return to the conversation in some specific time. If, as the apologist, you say, with exasperation, "I apologized, what else do you need?" you are just as likely to reenergize the conflict. Competence in the dance of conflict is the ability to hang in there, maintain your commitment to addressing the other's concerns (YCAMC). Hitting a wall is not an excuse to stop. It only means you have to keep listening. Discovering what's missing, you can offer it in a way that produces acceptance.

But forgiveness still may not be forthcoming. Even in the face of no forgiveness, apology stands on its own as a healing agent. You made your offer. It wasn't accepted. Declare yourself complete. You can bow and move on knowing that you did your best. Joy is still available – if you can find gratitude for the experience.

We have many opportunities beyond our intimate partners to practice forgiveness. My daughter, Lauren, 32 at the time, would not accept my apology for the pain she suffered when I did not immediately go to her side, prioritize her concern for my presence, when her father died. She told me, "I will never forgive you." "Really?" I asked, "Then how do we move forward in our relationship?" Her anger forced me to see that I had been incompetent at sorting out my priorities, and I was sorry for it. When she could accept that I failed rather than dismissed her, she forgave me.

If you can't forgive, you will make yourself ill by carrying around the pain that was inflicted on you. Maintaining your anger creates a persistent state of resentment and a constant hunger for retribution. Resentment, it is said, is like drinking a glass of poison and waiting for the other to die. You must find forgiveness – even in the face of no apology.

Forgiveness Without Apology

The process of forgiveness is fairly straightforward and easiest when you receive an apology. Sharing an understanding of what, how, and why the damage occurred from another, and receive damages, if appropriate, and commitments for the future, you can declare the debt paid. When there's no apology, you have work to do.

Sometimes, people don't know they are stepping on your toes. Maje, Cristián's 31-year-old daughter, was visiting us from her home in Barcelona. For people who need a lot of space, our one-bedroom apartment was tight quarters for a three-way dance. On this particular day, we had planned that she and her father would leave me alone to write in peace. Like many Spaniards, Maje has a very relaxed attitude about timing. For me, she was dawdling about, not taking my concerns to heart or making an effort to clear out. As the two of them were finally about to leave, she began a phone call with her partner and locked herself in the bedroom without any word. While I couldn't hear the words, I could tell she was fighting. Her father, waiting for her downstairs, was annoyed and kept calling me to ask where she was. Frustrated at my inability to focus, my anger was building by the minute. I intended to tell her how dishonored I felt when she came out. But in some moment, I observed my anger at her as a separate, infuriating being. Considering the situation from the 'we,' I could see through her eyes and I felt her pain. Compassion is the key to forgiveness. She'd had no clue she was stepping on my toes. When she finally exited the bedroom, all I could say was, "How are you?" Forgiveness comes easily when you come from the 'we.' I was then able to put aside my writing and have a conversation for ways of resolving her breakdown.

At times, our dignity and our continued relationship depends upon an apology from people who absolutely know they have damaged you and don't accept their responsibility for it. Without an apology, you're on your own to create a story that makes sense of the damage and why there should be a pardon. While it may not be possible to forgive the damaging act, it may become possible when you understand why it happened. There are plenty of examples of people who have forgiven heinous crimes by understanding the human beingness behind them. What's required is work to see the situation through the eyes of the one who is to be forgiven.

Why did it happen? What was the driving force? This is what you are called on to reckon with.

It's an incredible gift to yourself to find forgiveness for anyone who has hurt you and never owned it, dead or alive. Families, particularly parents who were raised in a different era and believe that having done their best means never having to say you're sorry, present frequent opportunities to practice forgiveness. While it's common in our society for people to completely divorce themselves from parents or other family members, it's not an easy (or desirable) thing. (Divorcing a family member is unheard of in indigenous communities.)

Both of my brothers have long harbored resentment about the way we were treated as children. Our father was absent thereby giving no practical enemy to push up against. Therefore, the brunt of the anger was directed towards my mother, who absented herself with alcohol and presenced herself with desperation, anger, and physical abuse.

My brother Cal often expressed a desire to write her off entirely. Most likely, with some semblance of gratitude for his life, he continued a miniscule relationship with her, maintaining distance for extended periods of time. In her advanced years, as she needed more and more help, he acknowledged the pain and unworkability of the situation and accepted my offer of help in releasing his anger.

I introduced him to The Scale of Competence and asked him to assess her in the domain of "parenting." She had always flown by the seat of her pants, without a clue as to how to lovingly care for and guide a developing child. Her only training for parenthood came from her own mother, who was extremely narcissistic and absent as a parent. After some consideration, it was obvious that our mother was blind to parenting as a domain of learning. We made many attempts to resolve our conflict with her, even in therapy, but she could never say, "I can see why you're angry."

The question he had to wrestle with was: Is it fair to hate

people for their incompetence? In grappling with it, Cal reflected on his own failures in raising his son, from whom he had lived separately since he was a child. If my brother was hoping for his son's compassion, he would need to begin by creating compassion within himself. Accepting his own incompetence made him a vulnerable human being and enabled him to forgive our mother.

I found myself in a similar situation where no apology was forthcoming from a damaging act. Two years after my second divorce, my ex-husband confessed to having had an affair with my best friend during the last year of my marriage. He revealed this in a therapy session. We'd sought counseling because, even though we were divorced, we still weren't complete. We hadn't been able to move on with our lives, occasionally getting back together for a night. We had never acknowledged our failures, apologized, or forgave. We needed to be radically authentic to be complete.

I was totally surprised by the information. And while I found it relatively easy to forgive him because he acknowledged the betrayal, my friend was a different matter. I felt doubly betrayed by her.

I had talked intimately with her while my marriage was falling apart and throughout the process of the divorce. Furthermore, I had hired her to come work in my new company AND moved her and her dog to my city. Unsurprisingly, our time working together ended badly within the year of her arrival. We hadn't spoken much, if at all, in the following year until I called her the morning following our therapy session.

I told her that I knew about the affair and was offering her an opportunity to clean it up with me. At first, she completely denied it – until I told her where the information came from, at which point she attempted to justify or excuse herself with these words, "It was another mindset." I have no idea what that meant, except that she declined the opportunity to engage with me in that dance of conflict. When confronted with the truth, she made no apology, which I found unfathomable and infuriating. In the two years after my divorce, I had been a whole, creative person, but in that moment, I had become a victim obsessed with justice. Months passed while I waited for her apology. I was burdened with an uncontrollable fixation. I was sick with resentment and dreams of revenge. Rage and righteous indignation were consuming my aliveness.

At some point, I realized that I'd probably be waiting forever with the pain. I had to find a way to let it go. No longer willing to carry the load and having been unable to sort through it myself, I put on my learning shoes and sought guidance. With the help of a good therapist, I discovered that forgiveness is the path of letting go.

The first step on the path was to acknowledge the chasm between us. I had her locked away in a distant cell. I needed to see myself in her and recall the 'we.' I could be righteous at the time, but in my younger years, I too had been reckless with sex and had affairs with married men. *Never with my best friend's husband,* I told myself, but this was just a way of holding myself above her. It was only by some good fortune that I never found myself in that situation. But it was clear to me that when I was engaged in sex with a married man, I had operated with zero regard for his wife. We really weren't so different.

In time, I discovered that secret affairs with married men don't work well for anyone. She obviously hadn't learned that yet. Was her lying worse than mine because she did it to me? Of course not. Accepting that reality, I could forgive her incompetence.

It's important to note: Saying, "I forgive," is often not a 'one and done' situation. Because anger may be triggered again out of the depths of unhealed pain, you are called to declare forgiveness anew.

It may be that the hardest ones to forgive are ourselves.

When the words are spoken, "I will never forgive myself for (fill in the blank)," you will either endlessly suffer your own slings and arrows, or you can find the lesson and make something of it. You suffer when you withhold your forgiveness. It produces a block in your aliveness. Your well-being improves by releasing it. Self-compassion comes easily if you embrace your failures and learn from them.

Unless and until you can declare, "It could not have been different," you're stuck, separate and judgmental. Accepting that reality, you can release the psychic debt that you've been carrying. Declare it complete. Be satisfied.

Forgiveness Is the Path to Redemption

Redemption – how you transformed the bad things that happened to you into something good – is an important component of your identity. Carrying old wounds makes you unattractive. Nobody enjoys being around someone who constantly dredges up historical inequities. Taking responsibility for your life means coming to terms with and finding benefit in whatever circumstances arose.

It took a few years for me to get enough distance to create a redemption story out of the betrayal of my best friend. Eventually, with a little time and space, I could see a chain of events that would never have happened had she not been my friend:

- She introduced me to Nichiren Shoshu Buddhism, where I learned about daily practice and how to tap into universal vibration.

- Through Buddhism, I met a famous TV actor who commissioned me to sculpt a portrait of his two sons.

- The actor asked me to teach Buddhist practice to a wild woman who introduced me to Ecstasy (MDMA).

The manufacturers were owners of a Mexican yoga resort.

- Through them, I met a woman who channeled the spirit of a 17th century priest named Father Andre. Father Andre told me to do the EST training.

- Through EST, I learned that I was responsible for my life and I met my friend Lisa; Lisa introduced me to Fernando Flores, who taught me the philosophy of language.

- Through Flores, I learned to be a learner and met Cristián.

- Through Flores, I also met the shaman who introduced me to the mountain that taught me about the interconnectedness of life.

The secret to redemption is to find the gift in your failures and pain and use them to become masterful in life. I bow to her, my old BFF, with gratitude for propelling me onto a path of learning, where I found my amazing partner. Without her, I wouldn't be who I am. I am eternally grateful.

Is there someone you haven't forgiven? Forgiveness is always possible, even for murder. If you're holding onto resentment, it means you haven't recognized the price you're paying. It also means you haven't yet taken responsibility for finding the conditions under which you can let it go.

Your ability to do this dance gives you the confidence to move in life knowing that if others have issues with you, you will be open to their complaints and deal with them in a way that brings you closer together. You can embrace those with whom you have great differences if you are willing to open your heart and invite them to a dance for mutually satisfying change and lead the way into the unknown.

We wage love and recreate passion when we attend to the challenges of conflict and disappointment. It is a gift of extraordinary proportion to be in partnership with someone who is willing to fail, apologize, learn, forgive, and return to a place of harmony and gratitude to life. If you can do this for yourself, you can lead others in an exquisite dance of relationship.

Journal:

The purpose of this journal is to focus on creating conditions for satisfaction and gratitude and liberating yourself from old wounds.

1. How enthusiastic are you to be with your partner on a Scale of 1-10?

2. What is in the way of a 10?

3. What are the activities that you love to share with your partner?

4. Do you wake up with gratitude for being alive and go to sleep with thanks for the day? If not, take one minute before rising and one minute before turning off the light and give thanks.

5. Consider the last time you spoke your appreciation and gratitude to your partner, your child, a colleague, or family member.

6. Dedicate time this week to do this: Express more than a "thank you;" share a deep expression of what you are specifically grateful for. Note what happened as a result.

7. When was the last time you heard an expression of appreciation or gratitude from your partner, child, colleague or family member? Are you willing to express your disappointment?

8. If so, make a critical assessment without blame. Start with, "Sometimes I feel unappreciated. Can we talk about that?"

9. Is there someone to whom you need to apologize? Will you? If not, why not?

10. Is there someone who owes you an apology? Can you ask for it?

11. Is there someone you need to forgive? Will you? If not, why not?

12. Is someone withholding forgiveness for you? Are you willing to bring it up?

13. Do you consistently share physical intimacy? If not, why not?

14. What fears or anxieties do you have about moving forward?

EPILOGUE

Becoming Together in Community

"The intuitive mind is a sacred gift and the rational mind is a faithful servant. We have created a society that honors the servant and has forgotten the gift."

–Albert Einstein

"Why can't we all just get along?"

–Rodney King

"If you think you are too small to make a difference, try sleeping with a mosquito."

–The Dalai Lama

"We must recognize that the suffering of one person or one nation is the suffering of humanity; that the happiness of one person or nation is the happiness of humanity."

–The Dalai Lama

W E FIND OURSELVES at a historical moment in time. Our society and our world have never been more toxically polarized and aggressive. Marriages are falling apart every 13 seconds. Gun violence is out of control. There is widespread cry for change, but few have any substantial ideas for accomplishing unity. We long for a sense of belonging – to someone or an organization that provides safety, support, and appreciation for individual gifts, real community. One of our biggest problems may be that we really haven't known how to honor difference and get along.

Indigenous cultures have elders who teach how to live together in peace and harmony. Western culture has no such teachers. Therefore, it is up to each of us to learn how to move with honor and create a life of meaning and purpose. Making a commitment to reduce your suffering calls for a serious commitment to become a better dancer in relationship. It's not about "them."

I have written this book to share a perspective on life that reduces suffering and increases joy. Feelings of isolation and anguish begin to diminish as soon as we consciously practice *the dance of love*. Learning the dance will substantially reduce the suffering in your life. And because we live in an interconnected world, your joy and suffering will extend to the rest of humanity. Seeing the dance of relationship and learning its moves is the answer to Rodney King's famous question, "Why can't we all just get along?"

If you've come this far, you will have recognized that everyone has the capacity to create love and that for love to endure, you must embrace conflict as the source of reunion and transformation. The dance is both simple and revelational, but just like the tango, you can't learn it alone. Sure, you can read a book, learn the mechanics and theory, and begin to practice by yourself. But you'll be limited in your development until you practice in the embrace of another. To learn, you'll need to practice with and get feedback from other dancers who have a passion for learning to dance gracefully.

Without feedback, you have little way of knowing what you must get better at. We must gather together with those who can mirror, guide, inspire, encourage, and teach us.

People who are committed to learn tango go to *practicas*, scheduled times in a dance studio with music, where people can come together for a few hours to dance. The challenge is this: The dance of relationship isn't being taught in schools. Because of its invisibility, there is yet to be a core curriculum on this most important aspect of human existence – relationship. Where can you go to practice?

Women's Conundrum in the Early 1970's

Women had endured a long history of suffering their lot in life. This started to change when they began to question what it is to be a woman and who said so. While the feminist movement began in the 1850's with The Women's Rights Convention, it wasn't until the cultural shift of the 1970's, propelled in part by the introduction of birth control, that it began to gather momentum. *Our Bodies, Ourselves,* one of the first influential works of women's liberation, came out of a meeting of 12 women sharing their personal experiences with doctors. Women were awakening to the fact that they have been defined by an invisible force called 'patriarchy.' It was becoming more and more of a problem to fit into an outdated profile that was in conflict with our own nature and desires.

At the time, there was no place to learn about womanhood. The possibility of redefining ourselves was an exciting and contagious idea that couldn't be explored in a vacuum. Since there were no "Women's Studies" programs yet, we would have to learn about being a woman in a new way. The women's consciousness-raising movement arose to address these concerns. Thousands of women began to meet in small groups all over the country, creating a safe space for women to investigate what it is to be a woman and grow. They were the backbone of the Women's Liberation Movement.

I hardly knew I had a consciousness to raise in 1973, but sitting in circle with other women, I began to see the box in which I was imprisoned. Meeting once a week for about a year, seeing ourselves through the eyes of other women, our collective consciousness, courage, and confidence expanded. Some groups still meet today.

Having reached this point in the book, you have undoubtedly recognized the extent to which you've been limited by your blindness to the dance and its movements. The dance has been as invisible as gravity was before Isaac Newton's *Laws of Motion* and patriarchy was before Elizabeth Cady Stanton's *Declaration of Sentiments*.

Now, more than ever, we are experiencing the cost of our blindness. The #metoo movement recently popularized on social media platforms like Twitter is awakening our need for greater relationship competence. Since this most fundamental of human skills hasn't been taught in school (yet), it's time to launch a relationship-consciousness movement with other like-minded people who know that something is missing and yearn for a more satisfying, respectful, and joyful existence.

Learning Together

While you now have an awareness of the dance, becoming graceful calls for practice with the moves with others who wish to become competent as well. Relationship practicas are those learning spaces. Following on women's consciousness raising (CR) groups, practicas provide a structure for sharing, learning, and reflection. Now, while it's wonderful to be physically connected with other learners, you don't even have to be in the same location to practice. In the 40 years since the inception of the women's CR movement, technology like

Skype, Zoom, GoToMeeting, and many others, has created virtual meeting spaces.

Looking at life from the perspective of the dance, you encounter a whole new set of questions to support you in defining yourself, your purpose, the qualities of a great life, and a path of action to be satisfied. Relationship practicas provide an opportunity, a structure, and a network of support and care for expanding your understanding of yourself as an individual and as a 'we.'

While women seem to have a greater inclination to learn together, don't write off men. It's beneficial to everyone to have a masculine, or, according to John Gray, Martian perspective. Inviting diverse people will naturally expand your vision of yourself and your world.

Commitment to relationship consciousness is the basis for community. As consciousness expands within the group, it overflows into individuals' larger family and communities. Connection with honor is the basis for a new world order. Peter Russell, a Cambridge University trained mathematician and theoretical physicist, sees this in formation.

In his book, *The Global Brain: The Awakening Earth in a New Century (2008)*, Russell compares the way individuals are beginning to link to form larger units to the development of the brain. In utero, once about 10 billion individual nerve cells have been created, they begin to connect to form the nervous system. Each of those cells has the inner wisdom to know where it belongs in life. In the same way, individuals around the globe are connecting, each innately knowing what the greater being will be, and looking for meaningful connection to make it so.

It makes sense that in an interconnected world the linking and grouping of individuals into larger units is creating an evolution of consciousness, better said, an evolution of heart. A new world order built on a respectful, inclusive way of living is being called for – a world in which we put our children and the elderly first, people get the love they need, and we prepare for the next seven generations. This is entirely possible when we learn the dance of relationship and live with a commitment to mastery.

Establishing a Practica

To start a relationship practica, you only need one other person who hungers for more heart presence in their life and is willing to make a commitment to meet regularly for at least seven sessions, ideally once a week for about two hours. (Good practicas can continue for years.) Bring one friend and ask your friends to bring a friend. More than two people is better, but ten is a good limit to the number of dancers lest the practice floor gets too crowded. It's important to keep the group small enough for everyone to participate. People need time and space in front of the mirror for reflection. If more people wish to join a full group, keep a list of their names. After meeting for four or five times, some members may feel comfortable to break off and start a new group.

The first meeting is an opportunity to get to know one another. This is a time to share some background about relationship. Are you married? Have you been? What do you do in life? What do you want to do? How are household responsibilities divided? How are conflicts resolved in your house? In your office? Do you have adequate support for your life?

Creativity flourishes in a place of safety. The role of the individual is to be a reflective mirror. The role of the group is to create a safe and compassionate listening space in which we can reveal failures and disappointments. Practicas do not require a leader although some may be facilitated by a therapist or a coach who is granted authority to lead by the group. In leaderless practicas, the group runs itself. Unless the group is facilitated by a trained leader, there should be no coaching, fixing, or suggesting. Questions can be asked for clarification about the moves that are being made. Without a specific leader, it's important to consider timing, how much you will allocate to each portion of the meeting. And it's effective to have one person monitor time and call out when there is a need for an individual to wrap it up.

Each member must commit to confidentiality and take responsibility for creating a satisfying experience. It is up to you to determine your conditions of satisfaction for your participation. Remember that you come to learn. Be dignified in your failures. Look for the lesson in each.

This book is a tool to stimulate discussion and action and support new thinking and change. Each member should have a copy and work through the journals.

The Basic 6-Step Format:

After the initial getting-to-know-you meeting, you may follow the structure below, going around in a circle, with each person speaking in turn.

1. **Check-in.** What's on your mind? Are you a 10? If not, what's missing? The purpose of the check-in is to bring dancers fully present, to clear distracting focus by getting concerns out on the table. This isn't the time for sharing the details and history of the situation. Set a time limit for checking in. Depending on the size of the group 2-3 minutes, max, is sufficient.

2. **Reflect on relationship activities since the last meeting.** What stands out as successes or failures? How satisfied are you with your work in the world? What frustrated you? Are your requests being fulfilled? Have you said YES when you wanted to say NO? Are promises being managed?

3. **Practice the moves by framing.** It's not enough to know what the six linguistic moves are. Proficiency is the ability to see them in the moment you are making them. Support one another by asking for clarification about the specific move they are making when speaking. Framing is stating the move up front; for example, saying, "My request is…" or "My assessment was…" The group's support lies in asking questions such as, "Is that an assessment or assertion?" or "Was there an opportunity to negotiate?"

4. **Today's topic.** It's useful to plan a particular focus. Choose one question from the journals at the end of each chapter, starting with, "What is your identity?" or "How has honor played in your life in the last week?" Each person speaks in turn with reflections. It is not necessary for each person to speak. Some people need to get comfortable. On the other hand, some people will speak ad infinitum, if allowed. There must be an agreement that it's OK to ask, "Where are you going with this?"

5. **Commitment to practice.** What you will do in the following week to build strength in the movements? Each person may commit to addressing specific areas of concern.

6. **Plan the next session's topic.** Use the journals at the end of each chapter as a guideline for your practicas.

Start your own practica or find an existing one on our website www.karenaberle.com. There you will find extensive videos and resources for continuing and improving the practicas. There is also space for you to share questions, experiences and insights to expand the consciousness of these learning communities. After meeting for several months, the group may want to start an action project, bringing relationship consciousness into a school or a nursing home, for example. Connect with us on the website to let us know where the relationship road is taking you. I am eager to dance with you!

"Never doubt that a small group of thoughtful, committed citizens can change the world. Indeed, it's the only thing that ever has."

—Margaret Mead

Further Reading

Bradley, Bill. *We Can All Do Better.* New York: Vanguard Press, 2012.

Gladwell, Malcolm. *Outliers: The Story of Success.* New York: Little, Brown and Company, 2008.

Gray, John. *Men are from Mars, Women are from Venus: The Classic Guide to Understanding the Opposite Sex.* New York: HarperCollins, 1992.

Hoffer, Eric. *The Ordeal of Change.* New York: Buccaneer Books, 1976.

Maturana, Humberto and Verden-Zoller, Gerda. *The Origins of Humanness in the Biology of Love.* Virginia: Imprint Academic, Philosophy Documentation Center, 2012.

Norsigian, Judy, and Boston Women's Health Book Collective. *Our Bodies, Ourselves.* New York: Simon & Schuster, 2011.

Russell, Peter. *The Global Brain: The Awakening Earth in a New Century.* Edinburgh: Floris Books, 2008.

About the Author

WORKING THROUGH THE crisis of a third marriage in tatters, Karen Aberle came to discover the *dance of love* as two vastly different worlds converged – the world of the intellect and the world of the heart. Her studies in the philosophy of language and apprenticeship in the shamanic tradition of the Huichol people of the Mexican sierra came together to reveal a roadmap for the return of tenderness, commitment, and passion to her marriage.

Karen has introduced *the dance* in a variety of environments over the last three decades. Through her leadership program, "Mindful Collaboration," she has coached people in Fortune 100 organizations to achieve extraordinary results by learning how to learn, love, partner, and fight – the same skills she and her husband have taught around the globe in their "Deep Relationship" programs for individuals and couples seeking more love in their lives. This book crystallizes their learning.

A native New Yorker, Karen now lives in Dallas, close to the embrace of her children and grandchildren. While she travels, speaks, and teaches extensively, you can always find her at www.karenaberle.com.

22001247R00086

Made in the USA
Columbia, SC
23 July 2018